SKILFUL WEIGHT LIFTING

John Lear

A & C Black · London

This book is dedicated to Al Murray, the father of modern weight lifting worldwide.

First published 1991 by
A & C Black (Publishers) Ltd
35 Bedford Row, London WC1R 4JH

© 1991 John Lear

ISBN 0 7136 3396 4

A CIP catalogue record for this book is available from the British Library.

Acknowledgements
Thanks to Andrew Callard, Heather Allison and Tony Supple for appearing in the instructional photographs; to Andrew Davies for his assistance with the 'Russian squatting programme'; to Mrs Virginia Price for her work with the text; also, thanks to Mr Jack Hynd for the photographs.

Typeset by Latimer Trend & Company Ltd, Plymouth
Printed and bound in Great Britain by Whitstable Litho Ltd, Whitstable, Kent

CONTENTS

INTRODUCTION

The aim of this book is to introduce lifters and potential lifters to the intricacies of technique and training of one of the world's oldest and greatest sports. It presents a stage-by-stage progression from beginner to champion and the teachings are based upon the scientific coaching scheme of the British Amateur Weight Lifters' Association (B.A.W.L.A.). This scheme was initiated by Alister Murray after the Second World War and whilst modifications and developments – especially in training methods – have been made, the basic principles of those inaugural stages are still retained; in fact, they have influenced coaching developments and schemes worldwide. Weight lifters owe a great deal to Al Murray who is truly 'The father of modern coaching' within our sport and I, as National Coach, am very conscious of his contribution.

B.A.W.L.A. is a highly sophisticated organisation which is able to offer training for all types of weight lifting in competition to the highest level. It is also the body which, through its Leaders Award, has established highly effective qualifications for fitness training based upon progressive resistance principles. In this way, B.A.W.L.A. is the leader in the health and fitness industry, proving valid qualifications based upon comprehensive courses in both free-weight and machine-weight exercise procedures and safety principles.

Whilst this book is concerned with the Olympic sport of weight lifting, those readers who work within sports centres and health clubs and gymnasiums should obtain qualifications from B.A.W.L.A. The principles outlined in this book for the techniques of lifting apply to all forms of resistance training. Study them carefully. Apply them to your training and the training of those whom you coach.

Enjoy a great sport through success.

Note Throughout the book lifters are referred to individually as 'he'. This should, of course, be taken to mean 'he or she' where appropriate.

EQUIPMENT

Weight-lifting apparatus: barbell, disc weights, collars, squat stands

Apparatus

Weight lifting is performed on a barbell which uses disc weights ranging from 25 kg down to 1.25 kg. In this way, a comprehensive range of weights can be made up at intervals of 2.5 kg. Smaller weights down to 0.5 kg are also available for use at record attempts.

The barbell itself, without any weights or collars, weighs 20 kg. This barbell is constructed so that the bar revolves from inside the end sleeves; this makes for easier lifting. The bar is precision built to ensure accuracy in weight. Knurling provides a good gripping surface. Barbells and weights are very expensive and few individuals will own such apparatus, but the majority of clubs will have a fully comprehensive range of weight-lifting apparatus.

Lifts themselves must be performed in competition on a platform measuring 4 m × 4 m (13 ft × 13 ft). The platform is generally made of wood, and rubber insets are included where the weight rests on the platform. Because of their heavy construction, platforms are not generally movable and, therefore, the club will provide a room specially for weight lifting.

Other pieces of equipment used, especially for assistance exercises, include dumb-bells, which are weights that can be used in each hand. Squat stands and racks which are height-adjustable will also be supplied. These are used when it is necessary to support heavy weights, such as in the performance of many leg and overhead exercises. Adjustable benches, inclined abdominal boards and leg pressing machines will also prove to be of value.

Boots and belt

Personal equipment

Any young weight lifter starting out in the sport should make a satisfactory pair of weight-lifting boots his first item of personal equipment. Suitable footwear will provide a flat, stable contact with the floor. As you will come to understand, balance is of the utmost importance and so the boots must afford a non-slip surface.

The lifter should also obtain a warm training suit. This will be worn during training and also during warm-up, prior to competition. It must be of such quality as to ensure that the lifter does not chill between his sets and warm-up exercises. At all times, it is essential to keep warm whilst training; whether you are lifting heavy weights or performing power or endurance fitness training, the musculature of the body will be under considerable stress.

Certain rules are laid down as regards to the clothing worn in competition. Generally, a leotard or special costume is worn, which must be of one plain colour. A T-shirt with short sleeves may be worn underneath it and club or national insignia may be carried on this costume.

Many lifters wear a belt. This piece of equipment has declined in importance since the press ceased to be a competition lift, but many lifters feel the need to have this tight form of strapping about the waist. The belt must not exceed 10 cm (4 in) in width.

All other personal equipment that the lifter wears on the platform is subject to the regulations of the International Weight Lifting Federation (I.W.L.F.) and will be checked by the technical controller during the competition.

All equipment must be kept thoroughly clean and in good repair.

Clothing: short-sleeved T-shirt (left) and leotard (right)

WEIGHT-LIFTING TERMINOLOGY

Assistance exercises These fall into two categories: technical assistance exercises and power assistance exercises. Often, aspects of both are combined and this will be illustrated and discussed in the chapter on assistance exercises.

Attempts and total The lifter is permitted 3 attempts at each lift. Between his first and second attempt the minimum increase permitted is 5 kg; between his second and third attempt the minimum increase permitted is 2.5 kg. The best result from the snatch and the clean and jerk attempts are added together to give a total. The lifter with the best total is declared the winner of the competition.

Bodyweight classes There are 10 bodyweight categories for men: up to 52, 56, 60, 67.5, 75, 82.5, 90, 100, 110 kg and over 110 kg. There are nine classes for women: up to 44, 48, 52, 56, 60, 67.5, 75, 82.5 kg and over 82.5 kg. The lifter must weigh-in within the limits of his class. (Lifting for schoolchildren frequently has the addition of 44 and 48 kg classes.)

Classical lifts The classical lifts are the snatch and the clean and jerk and are used in competition at all levels.

Clean and jerk One of the classical lifts in which the heaviest weights are lifted. This is a two-stage lift in which the bar is first lifted on to the chest. The lifter may split or squat underneath the bar in this first part of the movement. Having then stood up, the lifter jerks or drives the weight to arms's length over the head and may split his feet in lowering his body under the bar.

Clean and jerk grip Width of grip suitable for cleaning and jerking the weight. Means of deciding the width of grip for snatch and clean and jerk is discussed on page 14.

Elbow touch Touching the elbows on the knees in the squat clean – a cause for disqualification.

Hook grip Here, the thumb is placed along the bar and the fingers are then wrapped around it, squeezing it against the bar.

Intensity To find the average intensity at which you have been working, divide the work-out tonnage by the total number of repetitions for the work-out. The same method can be employed to find out the intensity for each individual lift or exercise.

Knee touch Touching the knee on the platform during the execution of the split – a cause for disqualification. This applies to the technique of split snatching and cleaning.

Lifting from blocks Similar to the hang, but the lifter takes the weight from blocks of varying heights and completes the movement. Both lifting from the hang and lifting from blocks require very careful coaching as there is a tendency to try to overcome the inertia of the bar by throwing the shoulders backwards and 'leaning' on it.

Lifting from the hang Here the bar is held in various positions such as knee height or mid thigh; from a static start, the lifter then completes the movement.

Loading This relates to both volume and intensity. Thus the loading may be light or heavy.

Maximum upward extension The lifter has made a maximum effort to lift the bar as high as possible with the full extension of the legs, body and shoulders, at the top of the pull.

Normal grip Fingers wrapped round the bar, with thumb outside fingers.

Programmes Composite plans directed towards a specific goal or competition. These may be of a long- or short-term nature.

Pull This refers to the lifting of the bar from the platform to a position of maximum extension prior to the drop. This term itself is unsatisfactory in the sense that the general understanding of pulling implies the bending of the arms – this is not the case in the weight-lifting pull.

Repetitions The number of times an exercise or lift is performed without stopping.

Schedule A plan of prescribed exercises showing sets, repetitions and weights to be handled.

Set A group of a specified number of repetitions. For instance, 3 sets of 5 repetitions is written as '3 × 5'.

Snatch One of the classical lifts in which the bar is lifted over the head on two straight arms in one continuous, dynamic movement. The body is lowered under the bar using either the split or squat technique.

Snatch grip The width of grip suitable for the snatching of weights.

Split-drop The lifter lowers or drops his body under the weight by splitting the legs fore and aft.

Squat-drop The lifter lowers or drops his body under the bar by sitting down in a squat position under it. The feet are jumped out to the side and the knees are turned out.

Starting position The starting position is considered to be the position of the lifter at the moment the bar leaves the platform. This moment may commence from a static start – where the lifter is motionless prior to lifting the weight – or as a part of a dynamic start – where the lifter has performed some preliminary movements to assist in overcoming the inertia of the barbell.

Straps Thongs of leather or webbing material attached to the lifter's wrists and wrapped around the bar, thereby enabling the lifter to handle very heavy weights without fear of losing his grip. Straps **may not** be used in competition, but are for **training purposes only.**

Tonnage Many schedules and training plans are based on tonnage principles. This is quite simple to follow and means the total amount of weight that is lifted in a training session. At different times of the year – depending on the distance from major competition – varying amounts of tonnage may be handled in each work-out. The tonnage may also vary in certain plans from one work-out to another within the week. In order to calculate the tonnage for each work-out, add up everything that is lifted in that session – i.e. all the weights multiplied by the repetitions for each set.

Volume The quantity of work in a work-out, which may be expressed in terms of number of lifts.

Straps are for training purposes only and may not be used in competition

MECHANICAL PRINCIPLES OF TECHNIQUE

Basic principles

The objective of weight lifting is to exert maximum force in order to overcome maximum resistance by means of certain prescribed technical movements. These movements refer to the two lifts used in international competition, the snatch and the clean and jerk.

In order that these lifts may be performed successfully, the weight lifter and his coach will be concerned with the development of physical, technical and psychological preparation, involving a thorough understanding of the technical and tactical implications of the sport.

In this section, we shall be concerned mainly with the technical development of the beginner and in the creation of suitable training methods.

The basic principles of technique are standard to all weight lifters, irrespective of their size. These techniques relate to certain mechanical ground rules which are unlikely to change in any marked degree unless there is some profound alteration to the rules of the sport. The primary concern is to lift the greatest weight above the head either in a single-stage movement, as in the snatch, or in a two-stage movement, as in the clean and jerk. Great mechanical efficiency will be required to accomplish this, especially in the following important areas:

1 maximum power development
2 balance
3 the ability to follow the 'line of least resistance'.

The latter two are of particular importance in the evolution of technique and it is necessary to develop a correct understanding of technical fundamentals from the very earliest days of a lifter's training. It is also the duty of both the coach and the lifter to adopt a disciplined approach to training regimes, from the outset.

Before looking at the technique of each lift in detail, it is important to study the problems of balance and mechanics further. Often, the positions through which the lifter must pass during a lift are not those which would seem to be natural in endeavouring to exert maximum force. The difficulty, however, is that frequently those movements that seem to be natural, such as endeavouring to lean one's bodyweight against the resistance as in the tug-of-war, are wrong and lead to serious errors in technique that, once initiated, cannot be corrected.

Remember that an experienced lifter may become victim to the errors that the handling of very heavy weights may present. Bad habits, once formed, cannot be broken easily. It is frustrating that even after much correct coaching, when faults may appear to have been eliminated, there is always the danger that a lifter would, under stress and pressure, revert to a beginner's 'traits'. If the early training has been poorly constructed, technical deficiencies will have been encouraged.

Olympic lifting is unlike many other power activities in that, due to the increase in weight between attempts, the circumstances change dramatically. In order to win a competition, it may be necessary to attempt weights which the lifter has not approached before, e.g. in order to secure first place, the competitor may be compelled to take world record attempts.

Under such conditions, the technique of the lifter must not fail him. It is an unfortunate fact that many lifters do not achieve the full potential that their strength levels would indicate due to a poor or undeveloped technical ability. Some lifters, on the other hand, because of their great fighting spirit and determination, become champions in spite of their technical flaws. It should be the objective of the coach to produce the complete weight lifter by marrying high standards of technical proficiency with a progressively developing programme of power training.

Balance

Balance is the most important aspect of any skilled activity. Unless we understand the principles of this and the least line of resistance, we may not be able to employ our strength in the most effective manner.

Every object has a centre of gravity; as long as this centre of gravity falls within the base of the object, it will be said to be in balance. With regular, inanimate objects it is easy to determine where the centre of gravity may be located. But when, as with the human body, the shape may be changeable, then determining the point of the centre of gravity will be more difficult.

When the human body is standing to attention, the centre of gravity will be within the body at approximately navel height, falling vertically over the feet. In this example, the feet, from toe to heel, are the base; as long as the centre of gravity is within that base, the individual will remain in balance.

If the lifter leans forwards from the ankles, the centre of gravity will shift towards the toes; as long as this remains over the base, the lifter is still in balance. Once he leans too far forwards and the centre of gravity falls outside the base, then he will fall over.

It is important to remember that once a lifter is out of balance, his chances of effectively utilising his strength diminish very rapidly. The lifter changes the position of his centre of gravity in relation to his base and, indeed, at the top of the pull, when he is up on his toes, his base has shrunk considerably.

The problem is further complicated by the fact that he is endeavouring to deal also with an object other than his own body. This is, of course, the barbell. Whenever there are two objects connected, our concern must be with the combined centre of gravity.

Combined centre of gravity

Assume that the weight lifter has stepped up to the barbell, has grasped it in his hands and is in the starting position, preparing himself to make the lift. At this stage, we are able to refer to the centre of gravity of the lifter and that of the barbell as separate entities. But the moment the lifter begins to exert force and lift the bar from the floor, we are then concerned with the **combined** centre of gravity of the barbell and the lifter.

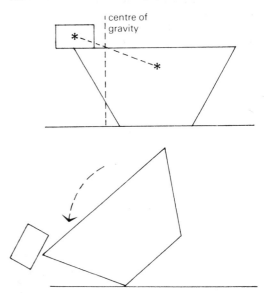

Fig. 1 Once the combined centre of gravity falls outside the base, balance is lost

In fig. 1, the centre of gravity is shown towards the heavier part of the object. In this case, the centre of gravity of the 25 kg up-turned weight is closer to the top than to the bottom, but falls over the centre of the base. When a small metal container or cup is added to one corner of the weight, the centre of gravity of this cup and the weight are now combined; this combined centre of gravity will move towards the cup since this is now the heavier corner of the weight. As material is added to the cup, thereby increasing the weight at that end, so the combined centre of gravity will move further up and towards the cup until eventually it will fall outside the base of the weight, which will topple over.

Similarly, when the lifter places his feet under the bar and bends down to grasp it, the forward angle of the shins from the ankle-joint and the height of the barbell from the floor, force the barbell to lie over the foot at a point where the toes and the body of the foot are joined. This, in fact, is towards the front of the base (toe to heel). Assuming that the lifter is reasonably proficient, the weight of the barbell is likely to be greater than his own bodyweight, and in some cases very much greater.

Now the combined centre of gravity will be towards the heavier part of the object – the barbell – and there will be a strong tendency for the lifter to be pulled off balance towards his toes. This will prevent him from exerting maximum force at the crucial point, as he is endeavouring to overcome the inertia of the barbell.

It becomes obvious, therefore, that the bar cannot be lifted in a vertical line from the floor but must be brought back towards the lifter at this stage, in order to bring the combined centre of gravity of bar and lifter over the centre of his base. This being achieved, the lifter maintains his balance and, therefore, his ability to use his power effectively. Thus, lifters should be taught to ease the bar back in towards the shins as it is lifted from the floor, so that by the time it is at knee height it is over the centre of his base (see fig. 2). This must be a deliberate technical instruction to all lifters.

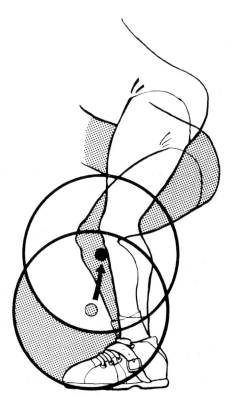

Fig. 2   The lifter must ease the bar back towards the shins as it is lifted from the floor, so that by the time it is at knee height it is over the centre of the base

Least line of resistance

In endeavouring to overcome the inertia of any heavy object, one of the simplest forms of machine that can be used is the lever. In fig. 3a, the weight that has to be moved is greater than the strength potential of the lifter. By placing a long rod under one corner of the weight and another object (the 'fulcrum') in the centre of this rod, the lifter will expect to be able to move the weight by exerting force at the opposite end of the lever.

The distance between the weight and the fulcrum is called the 'weight-arm' and the distance between the fulcrum and the point where the force or power is exerted is called the 'power-arm'.

If the weight weighs 100 units and the force exerted at the point of power is also 100 units, the lifter will be unable to move the object for it will be necessary to exert a greater force at the point of power. This can be achieved by following progressive training programmes, thereby increasing the power potential of the athlete. For example, with the technically limited movement of the dead-lift, the lifter may be able to lift, as an absolute maximum, in the region of 230 kg. In order to better this he must follow a sound training programme; hopefully, he may be able to lift 235 kg. Training will increase his lifting success.

It may not be possible for an increase at the power point. However, by moving the fulcrum closer to the weight, the critical weight-arm is reduced and so much greater mechanical efficiency can be developed (see fig. 3b).

As far as we are concerned, the weight corresponds to the barbell and the levers represent the long bones of the body and the spine. Whilst the spine is made up by a number of bones, we shall deem it a solidly constructed area – a flat, strong back is coached in all weight-lifting movements. The joints are the fulcrums and the points of power are the areas where the muscles are attached to the bones.

In all weight-lifting movements where the objective is to develop as much mechanical efficiency as possible, the fulcrums or joints are always moved towards the weight. Any attempt to move the weight towards the fulcrums sets up paths of directions (both for bar and body) which make correct technical lifting extremely difficult to achieve. Remember – the weight is heavier than you and it can very easily take control.

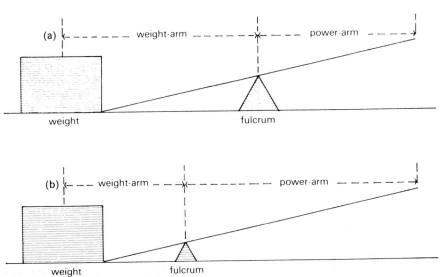

Fig. 3 Greater mechanical efficiency is obtained in (b) by moving the fulcrum closer to the weight, thereby reducing the weight-arm

In fig. 4, the barbell has been lifted to knee height and is moving through an area of mechanical and anatomical disadvantage. This region is called the 'middle range' and in all weight-lifting and weight-training movements, one invariably encounters greatest difficulty in this area. At this particular point, since there are several fulcrums in operation (i.e. ankle, knee, hip and shoulder-joints), we must decide which, in fact, is the 'active fulcrum' which must be moved towards the weight. Since the legs are virtually straight, the choice lies between moving the shoulders back, or hips in and up, towards the vertical line through the weight.

Let us take the first choice of the shoulder-joint. In endeavouring to straighten out the body against the resistance, it would seem natural to pull the shoulders back strongly. Unfortunately, this action causes the lifter to lean away from the bar and, in consequence, to pull the bar backwards, making control very difficult. It also limits the upward lifting potential. Here is an example where the natural movement that the lifter wishes to perform is, in fact, a serious mistake.

The active fulcrum is, therefore, the hip-joint. This joint must be forced in and upwards towards the weight, thereby reducing the weight-arm between the joint and the vertical line of resistance. This allows the lifter to achieve a position of maximum upward extension, thereby permitting him to exert maximum lifting force for the longest effective time. The shoulders will be seen to move from their forward position when the bar was at knee height to a position over the bar at the top of the pull. This backward movement is a reaction to the action of the forward hip drive.

Lifters are given the coaching advice 'Get your hips in and up to the bar'. In fact, what the coach is telling the lifter to do is 'Reduce the weight-arm that exists between the fulcrum and a vertical line through the weight by forcing the fulcrum in and upwards towards the weight'. By that means reducing the weight-arm, greater mechanical efficiency will be obtained.

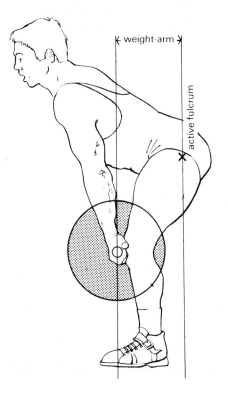

Fig. 4 When the bar has been lifted to knee height, it is moving through the 'middle range'. The active fulcrum is the hip-joint

THE TECHNIQUE OF THE CLASSICAL LIFTS

General principles

The technique of the snatch and the clean and jerk is based upon the mechanical principles that we have discussed previously in combination with the physical qualities of agility, a high degree of flexibility and the ability to express very high degrees of power. It must also be remembered that technique should not be considered in isolation as a mechanical phenomenon only, but that these other physical elements are essential in its mastery. Whilst some lifters may be technically very efficient but comparatively weak and others very strong but technically inefficient, neither group will achieve the highest possible results. So it is important to realise that technical development is an on-going process and that whilst there are certain standard technical essentials, the implications change as one develops and is able to lift greater weights.

In putting the shot, for example, the athlete – though he may encounter variations in throwing surface, weather conditions and so on – is still only concerned with the 7 kg weight for all his attempts. The weight lifter, however, although he too may encounter various qualities of platform, different makes of barbell and changing environment between one weight-lifting hall and another, has in addition to overcome the very considerable problems of changing resistance between all his attempts.

It may be necessary for him to enter entirely unknown areas where he may be expected to establish new records in order to win the competition. It is at such times that the lifter's technique must not break down and that his previous training must ensure that he is able to exert maximum force on a background of sound and unchanging technique.

In many other aspects the weight lifter and the shot putter require very similar physical attributes, but in this one area of changing circumstance, the lifter has greater problems. As with other highly technical athletic activities, it is the duty of the coach in dealing with beginners especially to insist that a correct technique is learned from the very earliest stages and is then maintained and developed throughout the weight lifter's career.

Many lifters are far stronger than their technical abilities will permit them to demonstrate. In weight-lifting terms, the easy part lies in 'getting strong'. The difficult part is being able to relate that strength to the highly athletic activities that are demanded by the snatch and the clean and jerk.

Grip

The first thing that we must consider is the difference between the width of grip employed in the two classical lifts.

In performing the snatch, the weight must be taken from the ground to above the head in one movement, whilst lowering the body under the bar, either by means of the squat or the split technique. In the early days of modern weight lifting it was realised that the wider the grip on the barbell, the lower the height it had to be lifted. Consequently, many lifters employed extremely wide grips with their hands touching the inside collars of the barbell. Whilst an advantage could be obtained in the form of having to lift the bar a smaller height, the great disadvantage was that the wider grip diminished the force potential of the pull; it was well known that the most efficient pulling position was with the hands at shoulder width apart.

Considering the two requirements of lesser height and strongest possible pull, basic principles of mechanics had to be employed to arrive at a satisfactory and effective position for the hands on the barbell. This is achieved in the following way. The lifter, standing erect, holds the upper arms horizontal. The distance from elbow-joint to elbow-joint across the back is measured and is then marked on the barbell with chalk. The lifter then grips the bar so that these marks lie between the first and second fingers – see fig. 5.

There are certain basic similarities between the snatch and the clean and these can be broken down into three stages of the lift, as follows.

1 Starting position leading to full extension; this is referred to as the 'pull'.
2 Transitional movement.
3 Receiving position.

Similarly with the jerk, where the bar is driven from the chest above the head, we will be concerned with four basic stages, as follows.

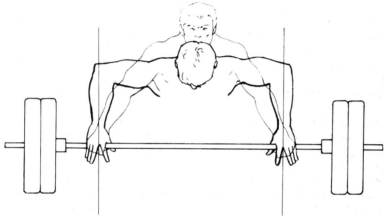

Fig. 5 With upper arms held horizontal, measure from elbow tip to elbow tip across the lifter's back; mark this distance on the bar. The lifter should grasp the bar so that these marks lie between the first and second fingers

Accepting that the wide grip means a lesser height through which to pull the bar, we are confronted immediately by the problem of a weight-arm existing between a vertical line through the shoulder-joint and a vertical line through the point where the hands grip the barbell. The closer the grip, the less will be this weight-arm. By holding the upper arm horizontal to the ground, a weight-arm exists between the elbow-joint and the shoulder-joint (with the forearms hanging vertically) that will be the limit of this particular disadvantage. Should the hands be taken out wider than this, the weight-arm will increase and the ability to exert maximum force will diminish. It is possible, however, to have a slightly narrower grip and obtain greater advantage, but the ability to use this will depend greatly upon the flexibility of the upper spine of the lifter.

1 Starting position.
2 The 'dip'.
3 The 'drive'.
4 The transitional drop to the receiving position.

The pulling movement and the receiving position are dynamic. To advance from the starting position to that of maximum extension of the pull requires great power in overcoming the inertia of the barbell. Here, we must develop acceleration on the bar. This means a steady and continuous build-up whereby muscle groups are used in sequence, the one building up on the other; this is called 'summation of force'. The object is to obtain maximum upward extension of the body so that the barbell may be lifted as high as possible; once the lifter begins to move to the receiving position, the momentum developed by a correctly executed pull will continue to cause the bar to accelerate upwards. Often this pulling movement is broken down into sections. These are referred to as 'first', 'second' and even 'third' pulls. To do this is incorrect for it gives the impression that the lifting of the bar is made in quite distinct sections, whereas it must be a smooth and continually accelerating movement.

However, for the purpose of theoretical analysis, we can sectionalise the movement. I shall refer to the pull by breaking it down into certain key positions, but the coach should not convey this impression to the lifter. For instance, lifters have on occasion been told to lift the bar to the knee very slowly and then accelerate from that position. This acceleration is called the 'second pull' but it has created great problems. If the barbell is moving very slowly throughout the difficult position at knee height, the only really effective means of then developing considerable speed is to throw the shoulders back and lean on the bar. The consequent technical errors can be disastrous. In coaching the lifter, it is vital to convey to him that the pull is a smooth build-up of maximum force and efficiency.

The receiving position is one of great control and in order to ensure that this is so, the lifter requires the mastery of various gymnastic attributes. Firstly, he must be very flexible in all the major joint complexes, in order that he may achieve the lowest possible positions as are demanded in the handling of maximum weights. Secondly, he must be very strong in this receiving position, both to hold the weight and in the recovery. Thirdly, he must master the qualities of balance and bodily awareness.

In many instances with the beginner, these receiving positions are difficult to achieve, and there are special technical assistance exercises to help overcome these difficulties, discussed and illustrated on pages 29–32.

The transitional phase of the lift refers to the change that takes place from the force-exerting position of the body in the pull to the force-controlling receiving position. This is also referred to as the 'drop'. The body is weightless as the feet leave the ground and at this time can, therefore, have little or no control over the direction of the bar; nor can it participate in the lifting of the bar to any greater height.

Remember that the bar can only be lifted whilst the feet are in contact with the platform. The position that the lifter goes through during the drop will be very much controlled by the technique, satisfactory or otherwise, that has been adopted in the pull. It is obvious, therefore, that the pull will consequently affect the final receiving position; whilst mistakes may manifest themselves in the final receiving position, their origin will probably be in an error that has been made at some stage of the pull.

For instance, it is easy to see that a lifter has dropped the bar behind his head in the squat snatch or that the split lifter has fallen to one side or other. The coach must look to see where these deficiencies originated so as to be able to give positive coaching advice to eliminate the mistake at source. In order to do this effectively, two things must occur. Firstly, the coach must be able to give clear and simple advice; secondly, the lifter must understand this advice.

All lifters must have basic theoretical knowledge of their sport for this to take place. This is essential in the philosophy of coaching. Too often coaches give advice which is not easily understood and consequently not put into practice. The coach must try to impart understanding and not impress himself with his own rhetoric.

To this end it is important that the coach has a series of blueprints of correct technique in his mind's eye against which he will see and measure every lift. These blueprints refer to key positions. When you are coaching, try to make sure that the lifter is passing through these positions at all stages of the lift. Study them very carefully. As a lifter, you should try to develop a sense of how it feels to be in these positions at the various stages of the lift. Many of the assistance exercises will help with this development. The key positions are as follows.

The pull

Starting position. This refers to the exact moment when the bar leaves the platform. In watching lifters, you will see many different movements of the body take place prior to the lifting of the bar. With the exception of a few very advanced lifters, these movements are generally only effective as a form of psychological winding-up prior to exerting maximum effort.

The bar at knee height. It is essential that the lifter and bar move through the correct path at this very difficult position. It is a troublesome area because it is the middle range, where the lifter is suffering from both mechanical and anatomical disadvantage. Mechanically, the weight-arm between the active fulcrum of the hips and the vertical line through the bar is most difficult to overcome at this stage. Anatomically, there is a change-over from those muscles which straighten the leg to those which extend the body at the hip. Wherever there is such an anatomical change-over there is a weak link.

Full extension at the top of the pull. In order that momentum is developed, the lifter must aim for this full extension. However, this does not mean that the pull is continued indefinitely because there is a critical point where the lifter must change to the drop for the receiving position.

Transitional period or drop. As we have seen, the position of the body in this area will be dependent to a great degree upon the pull and will consequently affect the receiving position.

The jerk

Starting position. Here the lifter has recovered from the clean and is standing in a positive and dynamic position.

The dip. The position achieved during this movement will determine to a very great degree the success, or otherwise, of the jerk.

The drive. This is a dynamic upward thrust against the bar which gives a limited upward impulse with maximum weights.

The receiving position. Here the lifter has dropped under the bar using a high split and should be seen in a position of strong support under the bar.

All these key positions for pulls, receiving positions and for the jerk will be discussed in greater detail but it is important to remember at this stage that a lifter may not pass through or achieve these positions properly due to any or all of the following.

1 Lack of strength in any of the essential muscle groups working at any stage of the lift. Wherever such muscular weakness exists there will be a fall off in the total efficiency of the movement.
2 Loss of balance. We have discussed this earlier in some detail but remember that if the lifter is out of balance he will not be able to utilise effectively the power that is at his disposal.
3 Use of the wrong muscle groups at the wrong time, i.e. lack of co-ordinated muscular effort. This often results from bad coaching at the earliest stages, e.g. the lifter may be allowed to bend his arms far too early in the lift. This attempt at 'snapping' at the bar will lead to out-of-sequence muscle group effort and a considerable diminishing of efficiency.
4 Lack of full joint mobility. Essential positions cannot be achieved unless the lifter is fully flexible. Muscular injury is also limited when a condition of full flexibility is achieved. Remember the condition of being 'muscle bound' does not exist for the Olympic weight lifter.
5 The lifter may find great difficulty in the development of speed. Remember that whilst we agree that there may be some slow-moving strong men, there have certainly never been any fast-moving weak men.

THE TECHNIQUE OF THE TWO HANDS SNATCH

The two hands snatch is the first of the two competitive Olympic lifts. It requires that the lifter takes the bar from the platform to above the head, arms locked, in one continuous movement. The very nature of this motion means that the lifter must exert great power on the bar in overcoming its inertia and it is a lift in which great displays of speed and force are demonstrated. In addition, to overcome the greatest resistance the lifter must employ sound technique in conjunction with power. This means that the overall movement is complicated and therefore, as will be seen later, the initial learning stages are very important in the mastery of the technique. This technique must be related to power development and grounded firmly at an early stage of a lifter's career.

Weight lifting is a power sport which has the special problems of changing circumstances. By this I mean that there is a great difference between a first attempt in a lift, where the weight may well have been successfully lifted on several occasions during the training process, and the third or final attempt, where the lifter may have to attempt a weight never before lifted. This may be a personal record attempt or, at the highest levels, a world record. These circumstances can greatly affect the lifter in many ways. From a technical point of view, the increases in the resistance can break down the previously learned technique by affecting balance, mechanical position and by forcing the lifter to employ physical manoeuvres which, while feeling powerful, are in fact causing the lifter and bar to move incorrectly and which result in failure to control the weight. In addition, there is a considerable psychological pressure placed upon the lifter when there is an increase in the weight to personal maximums and above.

In every competition, external factors are liable to affect performance. These can range from the condition of the apparatus, the bar, the platform or the size of the hall. Similar conditions can affect the shot putter or discus thrower in that it may be wet, dry, windy, or the throwing circle may be slippery or dry; but the main difference is that in these sports the resistance that is being handled does not increase from one throw to the next. Weight lifting, therefore, has very particular problems; coaches will need to pay a great deal of attention to the learning stages of both the two hands snatch and the clean and jerk so that patterns of movement can be ingrained which will not break down under the pressure of the changing circumstances of weight increase.

Bearing the above considerations in mind and relating to the mechanical implications of lifting that we have looked at previously, we may now begin to build up the technique of the snatch. In modern weight lifting the technique that is taught is called the 'squat style'. This method of lifting is the most effective, it being economical of movement and technically simpler than the older and now virtually obsolete method – the 'split style'. All young lifters should therefore be introduced to this first method of lifting from the very beginning and, as we shall see, there are a number of well-defined learning stages that will be practised in the build-up to the whole movement. Whilst some initial difficulty may be experienced, due mainly to problems associated with lack of full range mobility in the major joint complexes, these problems will soon be overcome.

In the development of the technique of the lifts – both the snatch and the clean and jerk – we build up our study by breaking the movement up into critical or key stages. Since we are dealing with mechanical principles, the way that the lifter passes through these stages is indeed critical as far as the successful completion of the lift is concerned; the coach and lifter must be aware of and understand where the lifter should be in terms of body position and bar placement at each of the key positions. These positions should therefore be seen as blueprints in the mind's eye against which, in the coach's view, the lifter moves. This skill is referred to as 'developing an analytical eye' and comes with experience after seeing many thousands of lifts. But to have the theoretical knowledge will help in the development of this essential coaching tool.

It is often the case that coaches, even those who have been involved in the sport for many years, will only indicate to an unsuccessful lifter the immediate fault. This is **negative** coaching and the lifter will be only too painfully aware of the error. The art of good coaching is to be able to see where the mistake began to develop, from which critical stage of the lift the breakdown originated and then to be able to give **positive** coaching advice as to how to correct it and prevent it occurring during the next attempt. Remember that the initial error will lead to others in the sense that having made a mistake, another is then made in an attempt to counter the first and so on. On this basis it is possible to develop a 'technique of

mistakes'; the consequence of this is that the lifter will never achieve his full potential since the limitations of technique will never permit a true exploitation of his full power. Indeed, there have been many extremely powerful lifters, weak in technical ability, who have lifted less competitively than other less strong but more technically proficient lifters. The aim, therefore, is to develop a firm and correct technique that will hold up under all the difficulties of the pressures of hard training and competition.

The key positions

(1) The starting position

This refers to the position of the body and bar at the exact moment the bar leaves the platform. Often lifters will go through a series of preliminary movements when first gripping the bar and these are to be considered as purely part of a 'psyching up' procedure; what concern us are the movements from the moment the bar leaves the platform – this is the true start of the lift. Note that the lifter will have gripped the bar with a 'hook grip' (the lifter on page 20 is employing a shoulder-width grip) and will have a snatch-width grip on the bar (see page 14).

The snatch: starting position

Adopting the 'hook grip': grip the bar as shown

Then wrap the fingers firmly around the bar and the thumb

The feet are so placed that when the lifter looks down, the bar will be seen to be directly over the junction of the toes and the main body of each foot. This ensures that when the lifter bends his legs at the knee and ankle, the shins will come forwards and graze the bar. Remember that the shins are not pushed back against the bar at this stage – such an action would cause the bar to roll forwards as the shins advance, making the bar swing away from the lifter and pulling him forwards onto his toes with a consequent loss of balance.

The feet are flat on the platform so that the lifter feels the weight of his body directly over all of each foot. Weight-lifting boots are designed to give this strong base. The distance between the feet is approximately hip width, the toes either pointing out slightly or, better still, placed as nearly fore and aft in direction as possible. This width and forward pointing direction of the feet allow for the best possible direction of force upwards through the body as the lift is made.

The legs are bent, being flexed at the ankle-joint, the knee-joint and the hip-joint. These angles of flexion are important. The ankle-joint is flexed so that the shin just touches the bar whilst the feet remain flat on the platform. This range of dorsi flexion of the ankle-joint is very much controlled by the angle at the back of the knee-joint. This angle lies between 90° and 100°, depending on the size (or, more specifically, the bodyweight class) of the competitor, with the smaller men (those with shorter legs) being closer to the 90° limit, and the larger (longer-legged) lifter being nearer to the 100° limit. In both cases, however, these angles are indeed **limits**. Below 90° means that the lifter would be sitting too low at the moment the bar leaves the platform. The likely result of this is that the lifter starts to sit back and, consequently, power is directed backwards onto the bar. This backward direction of the bar is then almost impossible to control. If the start is initiated with the knee-joint at an angle greater than 100°, the legs are too straight and a great deal of the essential leg power will have been lost. The result of this is that far too great a load will be thrown onto the back too early. The lifter then is forced to try to 'lever back' against the resistance and this again can cause backward directional forces to be applied to the bar, with disastrous results.

The angle at the hip between the body and the upper front of the thigh is controlled by the width of grip; since we employ a wide grip for the snatch, the body will be more squeezed up and therefore in a less effective position than, for example, in the clean. Here, the closer shoulder width grip permits a more open and therefore efficient starting position in terms of power development.

The position of the back is maintained in a flat, strong position throughout the lift and, therefore, this position is established at the very start of the movement. Many beginners try to lift with a rounded back but this reduces the mechanical effectiveness of the back in acting as a primary functioning lever throughout the lift. The flat back position, incidentally, is essential in all lifting and is a basic safety technique that is taught in weight training, lifting in industry and in the home. Remember that 'flat' is not necessarily vertical – it can be at any angle. As we pass through the various stages of the lift, the angle of the back will change but the alignment of the vertebrae will maintain a 'flat back'.

The head is so placed that the eyes are able to look down about 1.5 m (5 ft) in front of the lifter. Do not press the head back hard as this

will tend to give a backward direction to the pull and keep the hips down in a sitting position in the early stage of the lift.

The width of grip and the method of hook gripping have already been described on page 14, but it is important to remember to rotate the elbows outwards; this will help to ensure that the bar is lifted in an upward direction and will also help to keep the shoulders forwards. Maintaining this forward position of the shoulders is crucial and this aspect of technique will be emphasised throughout the lift. A summary of the starting position is therefore as follows.

1 **Feet**   Hip width apart. Toes pointing forwards. Well balanced on all of each foot. The lifter should not feel himself forwards on the toes or back on the heels. In relation to the feet, the bar should be directly over the junction of the toes and the main body of the foot.
2 **Knees**   The angle behind the bent knee-joint should be between 90° and 100°.
3 **Back**   The back is fixed in a flat position, with the shoulders in advance of the bar.
4 **Head**   The position of the head should be comfortable, with the eyes looking down about 1.5 m (5 ft) in front of the lifter's feet. Do not press the head back.
5 **Hands and arms**   Grip the bar very firmly with a hook grip. Rotate the elbows outwards, which will bring the shoulders forwards.

(2) Bar at knee height

Before moving on to describe the position of the lifter and bar in the second critical position, it is important to consider what is happening to the bar and lifter from the moment of lifting. It must be emphasised that it is in the early stages of the lift that many mistakes are initiated; these may result in failure at the concluding parts of the movement.

As the bar is lifted from the ground, the major muscle groups of the legs are brought very strongly into play. The angle of the back is maintained with its many muscles working statically to fix this position. This means that as the legs push against the resistance and straighten, the hips and shoulders move up together. In the description of the starting

**The snatch:
bar at knee height**

position, it was pointed out that the bar lies over the junction of the toes and main body of each foot – in fact, towards the front of each foot or the base. It is logical to believe that it would be correct to lift a bar in a vertical line since the shortest distance between two points lies along a straight line. However, if this was to be done the bar would be too far forwards in front of the base and there would be a tendency for the lifter to be pulled forwards, off balance. Throughout the lift, effective use of power will only be achieved when the lifter is in balance. We have already seen that this is dependent upon the position of the combined centre of gravity in relation to the base. Since the bar is most likely to be heavier than the bodyweight of the lifter, a vertically lifted bar would pull the lifter forwards, off balance.

It is therefore essential to ease the bar back and in as it is lifted from the platform. This is possible since the shins move backwards as the legs are straightened when driving against the

weight. Beginners often fear that they will hit the lower legs with the bar if they do this and so they tend to lift the bar forwards and round the knee. This they can do since, when learning the lift, the weights are very light. Such a mistake must be corrected immediately as it can have a bad transfer effect later in a lifter's career.

The result of easing the bar back and in as the legs straighten and the shins move to a vertical position is to bring the bar close to the knees, ensuring that the combined centre of body and bar is over the centre of the base (the feet). This will mean that at a most difficult position in the lift the lifter will be in balance and, consequently, will be able to concentrate on exerting maximum power. In addition, the easing back of the bar produces the reaction of bringing the shoulders slightly forwards. This is beneficial in the sense that it helps to control and limit the strong tendency to try to throw the shoulders back and lean on the weight as the lifter passes through the middle position.

Whilst we use the term 'pull' for this first stage of the lift, the implication is quite different from that of a tug-of-war, where the athletes lean against the resistance. In weight lifting, the tendency to take the easier line and throw the bodyweight back against the weight must be resisted because this action is transferred to the bar and will set it on a backward and uncontrollable path.

It is established, therefore, that as the bar is lifted from the ground, it is eased back and in towards the knees as the shins move back into a vertical position. The hips and shoulders have maintained their critical positions but have moved upwards as the legs are straightened. The shoulders have, in fact, been kept slightly forwards of the bar and the back has been maintained in a flat, strong position. This movement has been the result of a very vigorous leg drive and the lifter has been brought to this second key position with the bar at knee height and close to the knees over the centre of the base.

As we have seen in the section on mechanics, the middle range of movements is often the most difficult to actuate and, with the bar at knee height, the lifter will be experiencing difficulty on two fronts. These problems concern areas of both anatomical and mechanical disadvantage. Anatomically, the problem is centred on the principle of 'muscular group takeover'. The legs, having lifted the bar to knee height, overcome the inertia of the bar and, imparting acceleration to its upward pathway, are now at the end of their drive and the next stage of lifting will fall upon the muscles of the hips and back. Whenever there is a takeover of one group of muscles from another, weakness can be found. There is a tendency to employ incorrect mechanical manoeuvres to assist in the more rapid employment of the muscle group which will now take over the responsibility for continuing the movement. This group will do so without loss of power, actually accelerating power development.

The mechanical problems are here associated with the reduction of the existing weight-arms. These weight-arms (which can affect the efficiency of the lift at this stage) are, firstly, that between the fulcrum of the hip-joint and a vertical line through the weight and, secondly, that between the shoulder-joint and the same vertical line. As has been described in the section on mechanics, greatest mechanical efficiency is obtained in a lifting situation when weight-arms are reduced as much as possible and this reduction is achieved by moving the fulcrums (the joints in the human body) towards the line of resistance (the gravitational pull through the weight). The question is to decide which fulcrum to move towards the weight. Should the shoulder-joint be thrown back towards the weight, the reaction will be for the feet to jump forwards and the lifter to be placed in a leaning position against the weight. This action will direct the bar backwards rather than upwards, limiting the height of the lift and making it very hard to control as it passes over the head. This is incorrect. The hip-joint is the fulcrum that must be moved up and in towards the vertical line through the weight. The reaction to this motion is for the shoulders to come back, but this must be controlled as will be seen in the description of the third key position. A summary of the second key position is as follows.

1   **Feet**   As for the previous position – flat on the floor with the lifter well balanced over all of each foot.
2   **Knees**   The angle at the knee will be virtually straight, with the shins vertical.
3   **Back and shoulders**   The position of the back will have been maintained, shoulders slightly in advance of the bar.
4   **Head**   The position is maintained.
5   **Arms**   Arms straight, elbows rotated out.

(3) Maximum upward extension

Having concluded that the active fulcrum in achieving upward extension of the body is the hip-joint, the lifter is coached to force the hips up and in towards the weight, at the same time controlling the reaction of the shoulders from coming back too vigorously. The longer the shoulders can remain over the bar, the more effective will be the upward pulling action at the top of the extension. Coaches may be heard telling lifters to 'Stay over the bar'. But this is not the most natural thing to want to do as it feels much stronger to lean against the weight.

The snatch: maximum upward extension

The tendency to do just this, however, must be resisted; coaching of this stage of the lift is aimed at minimising any such movement. The aim of the lifter is, therefore, to extend the body high onto the toes, close to the bar, with a final elevation of the shoulders. There is also a bending of the arms in conjunction with the beginning of the drop into the final receiving position, with the bar above the head.

From the starting position to knee height, the lifter is coached to ease the bar backwards, bringing it over the centre of the base at knee height. As the bar passes the knee, it must be lifted vertically. It is necessary to emphasise that the bar is lifted vertically and upwards and not forwards or backwards. Whilst this may appear to be obvious, mechanical errors at any stage of the lift can cause the bar to be directed out of line. By maintaining the shoulders' forward position over the bar (especially through the middle stages of the lift), and keeping the elbows rotated outwards, this upward lifting action will be achieved.

Remember that the backward easing of the bar from the starting position is converted into a vertical lifting action as it passes the knees. The lifter, therefore, forces himself up and into the bar, rising high onto the toes, with the head driving upwards and the shoulders elevated to the ears. In conjunction with the elevation of the shoulders, the arms will begin to bend, pulling on the bar. Any attempt to bend the arms earlier in the action will prevent the development of full extension and cause the lifter to 'fold up', shortening the pull and making him 'dive through the bar' as he drops into the final receiving position. A summary of the third key position of upward maximum extension is, therefore, as follows.

1 **Feet** High on the toes.
2 **Knees** Legs straight.
3 **Hips** Forced up and in, close to the vertical line of direction of the barbell.
4 **Arms** Beginning to bend, with a strong elevation of the shoulders, towards the ears.
5 **Head** Driving vertically upwards.

Maximum upward extension: high on the toes, legs straight, shoulders elevated strongly, head driving vertically upwards

The snatch: the drop

The drop is initiated by the lifter jumping the feet out to the side and very slightly back, at the same time turning the knees out

The drop

Having achieved the position of maximum upward extension at the top of the pull, the lifter moves through a weightless condition in which he can no longer apply force as he drops down and under the bar. The extended position of the trunk which was achieved in the pull must be maintained during this drop. There may be a tendency to try to dive down and under the bar, especially if the lifter is trying to move very fast. But whilst speed is an essential element of all weight lifting, it must be controlled; therefore, a fast drop, maintaining the upright position of the trunk, is essential.

This drop is initiated by the lifter jumping the feet outwards to the side and very slightly backwards, at the same time turning the knees outwards. Again, the importance of maintaining the upright position of the trunk must be

emphasised. The action of jumping the feet out and apart will allow the hips to be sat down in between the heels and this will also allow the upper two-thirds of the trunk to remain in an upright and strongly supportive position. The coach will often be heard telling a lifter to 'Sit in and sit up'. This means 'Sit the hips in close to the heels and keep the trunk upright'. The upright position of the trunk will place the lifter in a strong position to punch out against the downward resistance of the bar.

As the lifter sits into this low receiving position he will be slightly behind the bar, so it is necessary to bring the bar back and then punch it out vertically as it comes over the head. This control of the backward movement of the bar is vital and there will be great emphasis on the vertical component of the overhead placement of the bar in the full receiving position.

The snatch:
receiving position

(4) The receiving position

1 **Feet** Jumped out and apart, flat on the floor.
2 **Knees** Turned out and positioned over the feet, pointing in the same direction.
3 **Hips** The hips are sat down in a squatting position, close to the heels.
4 **Back** In the sitting position there will be a natural curve in the lumbar spine but the extended position of the upper two-thirds of the trunk, as achieved in full extension, must be maintained.
5 **Arms** Strongly locked out, straight above the head, supporting the bar.

The recovery from this low receiving position is most important because, with the bar above the head, the combined centre of gravity will be high and, consequently, any unnecessary movement fore and aft could cause loss of balance. The lifter should ease the head very

slightly forwards through the arms. This action will relieve pressure on the tightly compressed knee-joints and will give the muscle groups which extend the knees and hips a 'start' in their angle of pull in rising from the low squat position. Keep the knees out and apart throughout this action. Since the adductor muscles on the inside of the thigh tend to be stronger than the opposing abductors, there is a tendency for the thighs to be pulled together when rising; this will push the hips back and tip the trunk forwards. The lifter must resist this and keep the knees out as he rises. The same approach must be applied in all squatting.

At all times during the recovery the lifter must keep pushing strongly against the barbell. When stood erect, the feet should be stepped back, hip width apart, square-on to the front; there the lifter must remain, bar held above the head, until the referee gives the signal to replace the bar on the platform.

Teaching the snatch: the lifter must receive from the coach information that is clear, simple and easily understandable

Teaching stages

As we have seen, the snatch is a complex gymnastic movement, made all the more difficult by the changing circumstances of increasing weight from one attempt to another. It is also a very fast lift in which the technical pathways have to be accurate and the technique must be developed stage-by-stage in the learning process. This way, when the time comes for the lifter to display his athletic prowess, concentration can be directed at the development of power.

Undoubtedly for the beginner, the best introduction to the snatch must come from a well performed demonstration. For a coach to explain the technique and then provide a good demonstration himself is an extremely valuable experience for the young lifter. If this is not possible, the coach should use another technically proficient and experienced lifter in the demonstration-explanation process. Here the coach can highlight and develop essential coaching points whilst the lift is being performed. Television, video and films of great lifters are also very valuable, as are series of photographs illustrating all the stages of the lift. These visual aids serve to whet the appetite of the potential lifter and provide the initial pointers as to what will be expected in the performance of the lift.

Whatever techniques the coach may employ, however, it is essential that he gives clear, simple and easily understandable information to the student.

As far as the introduction of this lift is concerned, there is a series of exercises through which the young lifter should be led. These movements are called the 'snatch-balance exercises' and consist of graded stages, each a progression on the previous movement, combining the development of technique and great strength, speed, flexibility and confidence. In conjunction with these exercises, the lifter should be taught to lift the bar, making sure that it and the body pass through the key positions, to maximum upward extension. These positions have already been described and should be followed very carefully.

As the lifter becomes more experienced, this part of the snatch-pull may be continued through to the high power snatch, where the lifter takes the weight from the floor to above the head in one continuous, flowing and accelerating movement. This is performed with a short dip of the body in which the heels are dropped back to the ground and the knees and hips are flexed. The bar is punched vertically above the head in conjunction with this dip (see power snatch assistance exercise on page 51). This power snatch will help to give the lifter a sense of the full movement but it must be explained that in order to snatch the heaviest weights, the lifter must sit into the lowest receiving position.

First check the position of the feet so that the lifter can sit down in the full squat; the feet should be flat on the floor, with the upper trunk erect. This may be difficult in the initial stages but the snatch-balance exercise will develop the essential flexibility to achieve this squat position. If this is a problem to start with, the first exercise should be performed with the lifter being encouraged to sit as low as possible with each repetition.

Assistance exercises

Exercise 1

Bar position – Held above the head. Snatch grip.
Feet position – Receiving position.
Action – Squat down into the full receiving position. Remain in low position for a few seconds before recovering – this helps to feel the balance of the movement.

Exercise 2

Bar position – Resting on shoulders behind neck. Snatch grip.
Feet position – Receiving position.
Action – Press the bar above the head, at the same time sinking into the full squat receiving position. Recover.

Assistance exercises: exercise 1

Assistance exercises: exercise 2

Exercise 3

Bar position – Resting on shoulders behind neck. Snatch grip.
Feet position – Receiving position.
Action – Heave the bar above the head, at the same time dropping into the full squat receiving position. This is a dynamic movement. Recover.

Exercise 4

Bar position – Resting on shoulders behind neck. Snatch grip.
Feet position – Pulling position.
Action – Heave the bar above the head, at the same time jumping the feet to the receiving position as the lifter drops down. This is a very dynamic action, closely resembling the final position of the snatch.

Assistance exercises: exercise 3

Assistance exercises: exercise 4

Exercise 5

Bar position – Resting on the front of the chest. Snatch grip.
Feet position – Pulling position.
Action – Heave the bar above the head, at the same time jumping the feet to the receiving position as the lifter drops down. Recover.

Assistance exercises: exercise 5; rest the bar on the front of the chest with a snatch grip and with the feet in the pulling position

It must be pointed out that exercise 5 is advanced. Since the lifter is slightly behind the bar at the top of the pull, similar circumstances can be created by placing the bar on the lifter's chest at the start of exercise 5. As the lifter heaves the bar from his chest, he must learn to ease the body slightly forwards to bring himself under the bar to the correct and stable position of support in the full receiving position. Since even the best technicians tend to lean on the bar when it is very heavy, this exercise is very much a learning procedure for them as well as a valuable power builder. Even advanced lifters need to re-establish technique every so often.

It is essential to use assistants to help with the lowering of the bar back to the lifter's shoulders when these exercises are performed for repetitions. Do not advance from one exercise to the next until you are fully satisfied that the movement has been mastered. These exercises are used initially for teaching, but the more advanced sections are frequently used by experienced lifters to develop power in the low receiving positions and in recovery. Under these circumstances, very heavy weights can be used, frequently in excess of the lifter's maximum snatching ability.

The value of the snatch-balance exercises can, therefore, be summarised as follows.

1 Learning the full range of movement.
2 Developing the necessary flexibility in ankle, hips, trunk and shoulders to achieve the correct receiving position of support.
3 Developing a sense of balance in the low position with a weight above the head.
4 Developing strength and power in the low receiving position. This is especially so with exercises 4 and 5 which can be used as very important advanced power building exercises.
5 Developing confidence in the low position.

Assistance exercises: exercise 5; heave the bar above the head, at the same time jumping the feet to the receiving position

Assistance exercises: power snatch; starting position

Assistance exercises: power snatch; take the bar from the top of the pull to above the head in a dynamic fashion

The best advice to the coach who has responsibility for teaching the young is to build up this complicated movement through these balance exercises, never moving onto the next stage until mastery of each exercise has been established. In this way, a technique will be constructed that will operate under increases in weight and the other pressures inherent in competition. It is worth remembering that when under such pressures – both physical and mental – the lifter will rely on or revert to the first things learned. Should early teaching have been of a technically poor nature, then despite later more careful coaching and apparent correction of initially displayed faults, the circumstances of vitally important competitions are very likely to so pressurise the lifter that these early errors will dominate the lifting, with disastrous results. The coach and lifter must be disciplined in their approach. It is worth taking time.

In combination with the snatch-balance exercises, the lifter must be taught how to link the pull and squat. This involves a change of direction, as previously described, and a re-positioning of the body under the bar. This transitional movement is referred to as the 'drop'. Naturally, the balance exercises will have accustomed the lifter to the second part of the movement, but the change from pulling to receiving will be taught through the power snatch. Whilst this exercise is most frequently performed as a power developing exercise, here the emphasis will be on taking the bar from the top of the pull to above the head in a dynamic fashion, with appropriate feet movements as in the full receiving position. Initially, this movement will place the lifter in a high position, but as greater confidence and sense of balance is developed, so the lifter can sit lower and lower until such a time as he sits into the full receiving position and, in fact, completes the snatch. The control of the bar above the head must always be emphasised and a very positive approach to the action of punching the bar out above the head to full arm lock must be encouraged.

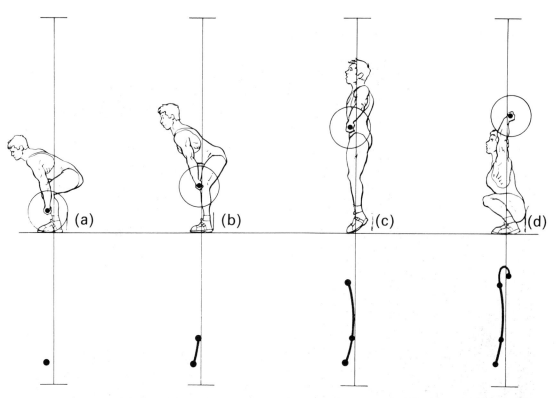

Fig. 6 Direction of the bar during the pull. Starting position (a): bar towards front of base due to forward angle of shins. Bar at knee height (b): as legs straighten shins move back, allowing bar to be eased in over centre of base. Full extension (c): bar carries slightly forwards as hip fulcrum is driven in and up. Receiving position (d): bar is taken back slightly to bring it over the lifter

Direction of the bar during the pull

It would seem logical that, based on the principle that the shortest distance between two points is a straight line, the bar ought to be pulled in such a direction. As we have seen in our study of the combined centre of gravity of body and bar, this cannot be the case in weight lifting since the resulting displacement of balance in relation to the lifter's base would seriously limit the efficient application of power and have a detrimental effect on the technical control of the lift. Benefit from or knowledge of the mechanical/anatomical parameters shows that the bar is, in fact, pulled in a shallow 'S'-shaped curve. As has already been explained, the initial inward curve of the bar's pathway results from a deliberate easing back of the bar to the knee as the shins move to a vertical position during the extension of the legs. The next, outward curve occurs as the hips are forced up and in towards the bar. This

movement of the bar must be controlled, however, and the lifter should be instructed to actually lift the bar vertically from the point where it passes the knees to the top of the pull.

This forward direction of the movement is accidental to the hip action; the necessary technique of maintaining the shoulders forwards through the middle range as long as possible with the elbows externally rotated, will help to prevent the forward swing of the bar becoming excessive. At the top of the pull there is a slight 'hook' on the bar to bring it over the head. Since this movement directs the bar backwards, it must be controlled and changed to a vertical drive as soon as the bar is over the head. If the hook is too pronounced and uncontrolled, the lifter can lose the bar backwards, behind the head. If it is made too vigorously, anatomical reaction can cause the muscles on the anterior part of the shoulder and the chest to contract as a reaction to overstretching and the lifter can be shot out backwards through the line of the bar. In both cases the lift will be lost.

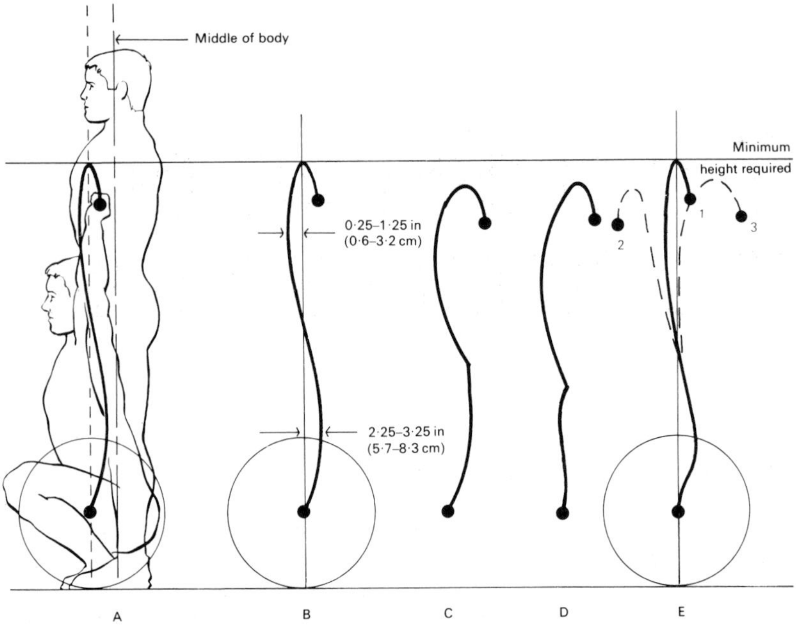

Fig. 7 Paths A, B and E1 fulfil basic criteria of line of direction for the pull. Paths C, D, E2 and E3 illustrate errors

Both coach and lifter should study fig. 7 carefully. A, B and E show the correct line of the bar; C and D show basic errors.

In path C, the barbell has been taken back at the start of the lift, but this backward movement is continued past the knees, pulling the bar in towards the hips. This brings the bar in far too close to the hips at the moment when the weight-arm must be reduced by forward hip action. The lifter is then forced into either:

1 an exaggerated forward swing of the bar in an effort to 'get the hips in', as is necessary for a full upward extension. This then demands that the bar be pulled back vigorously to bring it over the body, an action which is very difficult to control, or
2 a situation where the hips are fixed, with the shoulders thrown back vigorously and the barbell pulled back. This is a very common error – especially when the weight is heavy – since lifters will seek to gain power by leaning their bodyweight against the bar.

Both these errors result in considerable mechanical and anatomical disadvantage for the lifter since he will be limited in fully utilising his power source; it may also be the case that mis-directed power will cause the bar to control the lifter, rather than vice versa. The coach should try to stand at the side of the platform when the lifter is performing so that the path of the bar in relation to the movement of the body can be seen fully. This is especially important as

the bar passes the knees in the second key position. If the relationship between bar and lifter is correct at this stage, the chances of a successful lift will be greatly enhanced.

Path D shows the barbell moving away from the lifter at the start of the movement. This can be caused by the following.

1 The inexperienced lifter fearing that he will bang the bar against the knees which are set forwards in the starting position, thereby subconsciously lifting the bar round the knees.
2 Assuming the position over the bar when the legs are straight with the barbell pressed close to the shins; when the lifter then bends the legs in assuming the correct starting position, the barbell is pushed forwards and rolls away from the lifter.
3 Starting the movement with the seat too low.

The action of the barbell travelling forwards tends to pull the lifter off balance and onto his toes. The heavier the resistance, the more likely this effect will be. When the lifter is off balance he can no longer exert maximum force. In addition, there is an increased weight-arm when the bar travels forwards. The result is for the lifter to pull the bar back vigorously; again, this incorrect re-direction of the bar becomes uncontrollable.

Path E2 shows the bar to have been pulled forwards, usually due to an incomplete extension of the body. In path E3 the bar has been pulled back due to the lifter 'leaning' backwards during the pull.

THE TECHNIQUE OF THE CLEAN AND JERK

The second of the two lifts – the clean and jerk – is indeed the king of lifts; it is the great challenge of strength and athletic ability. In the past the press was always designated as the lift for the very strong, the snatch for the athletic and the clean and jerk for the lifter who was able to combine the qualities of great strength and athletic ability in one movement. The press has now been eliminated from competition and so the clean and jerk has taken on even greater importance in the nature of the sport. There are, therefore, two very sound reasons why this lift is especially important in competition.

1 Since the lift is in two stages, the heaviest weights can be handled. As a result of this, all the technical points that we have covered in describing the snatch are greatly emphasised in this lift. The lifter must remember that the increased weight that he must overcome will present an extra problem in maintaining skill and technique.

2 In addition, since it is the final lift in the competition, good results are vitally important. Often lifters may have to achieve new personal bests, at all levels, in order to win a competition. Louis Martin of Great Britain had to lift 12.5 kg more than he had ever lifted before in order to win his first World Championship when he beat the Soviet lifter Arkardi Vorobyev in 1959.

In many ways then, the problems are psychological as well as physical, for not only must the lifter overcome very heavy weights, but he must also deal with the problems of beating opponents and winning competitions.

In a theoretical study, the lift can be broken down into two parts, the clean and the jerk. In practical terms, however, it must always be thought of as a whole, with the jerk section being very much dependent on the efficient execution of the clean. Indeed, in modern terms the lift is referred to as 'the jerk', without reference to the clean section. In practical training activity, however, the lift is frequently practised as separate parts; a lifter may work hard on the clean on one day whilst performing the jerk from stands on another. In this way greater energy can be applied to each part.

Some lifters may find that whatever weight they can clean they will be able to jerk. For these lifters, extra work on cleaning may be necessary, involving both pulling and squatting. For others, cleaning may not be the main problem, but the difficulty will arise in jerking the weight above the head. This may be either a technical or a strength-related weakness and so appropriate extra work will be undertaken. However, when competition draws nearer, the complete lift will be practised as a whole and the lifter must remember that the easier the clean, the greater the chances of jerking the weight for a successful lift.

The clean

The first major difference between the snatch and the clean will be seen in the width of grip. When we studied the grip for the snatch (page 14), it was demonstrated that the closer the grip to shoulder width, the stronger would be the pulling position. Initially, therefore, young lifters are taught to lift with a shoulder width grip so that when the bar is resting on the shoulders, the inside edge of the hand on the thumb side will be level with the lateral surface of the edge of the shoulder muscles. For more experienced lifters, a slightly wider grip may be favoured, especially for those who have some difficulty in locking out on the jerk. Grips closer than shoulder width are not recommended as it would mean that the hand would be crushed against the shoulder by the bar.

When the lifter is viewed in the receiving position with the bar on the shoulders, he should have an open chest, held up, with the bar resting on the anterior shoulder muscles. The elbows are forwards and slightly upwards, ensuring that the bar is resting on a firm base. This position is maintained during the dip at the start of the jerk and will be the platform from which the bar is thrust during the drive. For all lifts the hook grip must be used during the pull. The hand can be opened after the bar has been received on the chest, releasing the thumb into a more comfortable position. The bar, however, must be gripped very tightly throughout the jerk.

We shall study the clean using the same reference to key positions as we did for the snatch. There are obvious similarities, with regard to which it is worth establishing that these are unalterable aspects of technique that must be fully understood and applied during all lifts.

The clean: starting position

The key positions

(1) The starting position

The feet are placed under the bar, hip width apart, with the toes turned out slightly. A view down through the bar places it over the main body of the foot and its junction with the toes. This means that the bar is to the front of the base. The lifter must feel that he is standing evenly on all of each foot, not with his weight forwards on the toes or back on the heels; this will ensure that he is well balanced at the start of the lift. He grasps the bar with a hook grip and a shoulder width hand spacing as has been previously described. Maintaining the back in a strong, flat position, he bends at the knees and hips, lowering the body down. The angle at the back of the knees will be between 90° and 100° (depending upon the height of the lifter); this range ensures that the hips are higher than the knees. Should the lifter have an angle of less than 90° at the start of the lift, he is sitting too low and the direction of the pull is then likely to be backwards, with the lifter leaning on the bar. An angle greater than 100° means that the legs are too straight and essential leg drive will be lost, too much resistance being thrown on the back. Since the lifter has a shoulder width grip, the angle between the chest and the top of the thighs will be more open than in the snatch. This is, in fact, to the lifter's advantage.

In this position, the elbows should be rotated round and outwards, ensuring that they follow an upward direction as they begin to bend at the top of the pull. Throughout the earlier part of the pulling movement, this action also helps to keep the shoulders forwards. This position is, of course, particularly important as the lifter passes through the middle range of the movement. The arms are straight in this position and the novice lifter must be coached to maintain them as such because, until the very top of the pull, they are merely connectors between the main power source of legs and body. Any attempt to bend them too soon against a heavy resistance will 'kill the pull' – rather than lifting the bar, the tendency will be to stop the upward movement of the back. The legs, however, are likely to continue to straighten.

The lifter can be left in a straight-legged dead-lift position with the bar too low and with great resistance thrown onto the back; this compels him to lever back against the bar in an attempt to maintain the lifting momentum. As we saw in the section on mechanics, an effective build-up of power stems from a correctly linked path of muscle activity, from the largest groups overcoming inertia to the smaller ones building the momentum at the top of the lift. The arm-bending action being applied by comparatively small muscles must function correctly at this stage of the lift.

The starting position is essentially dynamic; the lifter gathers all his strength and technical potential in preparing to overcome the inertia of the bar. It must be remembered that, here, we are referring to the exact moment the bar leaves the platform. Many experienced lifters may go through a series of movements prior to lifting the bar. Whilst such movements may help in the build-up of concentration and a positive approach, the technique of the lift begins as the bar leaves the ground. Novice lifters should be taught to lift directly from the platform, without these prior movements.

A summary of the starting position is as follows.

1 Feet Hip width apart, toes pointing as near fore and aft as is comfortable. Feel the weight of the body on all of each foot, from toe to heel.
2 Knees The angle at the back of the knees is between 90° and 100°, depending on the size of the lifter. The description of this is the same as for the snatch.
3 Hips Because of the closer hand grip, the angle between the top of the thighs and the chest and abdomen is more open. This is an advantage because the lifter is not so compressed in the starting position.
4 Back The back is flat. Remember 'flat' can be at any angle, not necessarily vertical.
5 Shoulders Slightly in advance of the bar.
6 Head Keep the head in a comfortable position in relation to the angle of the back. Do not press it back hard as this will give a backward direction as you start to lift. The eyes should be looking down, about 1.5 m (5 ft) in front of the lifter.
7 Hands Grip the bar very firmly, employing a hook grip (shoulder width), with the elbows

rotated outwards. This position will help to maintain the forward position of the shoulders.

(2) Bar at knee height

As has been described, the position of the bar in the starting position is to the front of the base, over the junction of the toes and the main body of each foot. When the lifter bends down, the shins will come forwards and graze the bar without rolling it forwards. Should the lifter attempt to lift the bar in a vertical line, however, he would most certainly be pulled forwards, off balance. At the moment of lifting, we are concerned with the combined centre of gravity of body and bar and as this will always move to the heavier part of the object, i.e. the bar, it is essential that it is brought over the centre of the base as soon as possible. It is important to remember that if the lifter senses that he is out of balance, he will no longer be able to concentrate on exerting maximum power.

As the bar is lifted from the floor we have two concerns; firstly, that the body and bar are so positioned that the lift can benefit from the greatest mechanical efficiency and, secondly, that resulting from the mechanical considerations, the largest and most powerful muscles of the body, i.e. those of the legs and hips, can be brought into play to overcome the

The clean: bar at knee height

inertia of the bar and to develop momentum gradually.

The action of these muscle groups will straighten the legs and the shins will move back so that a path is opened up to allow the bar to be eased back as it is lifted. By the time it is at knee height, it will be close to the knee and over the centre of the base. This action will keep the lifter in balance and prevent him being pulled forwards by the weight. As he passes through this stage, the back will be maintained flat and the shoulders forwards – in fact, in the same position as that from which he started.

Coaching the lifter through this first section of the lift is most important. Much depends upon the position of body and bar in this second key position. At this stage, the weight-arm between the active fulcrum of the hip-joint and the vertical line of force down through the bar is critical. The lifter may try to get past this stage by manoeuvres which, whilst seeming to help, will in fact set up body directions which will transfer to the bar and break down technique. Most frequently, this is seen when the lifter fixes the hips and throws the shoulders back against the resistance of the bar. Great discipline is required to prevent this mistake occurring and the coaching advice of 'Keep the shoulders forwards' or 'Stay over the bar through the middle position' is most positive. The action of easing the bar back to the shins helps because the reaction to this movement is for the shoulders to come forwards slightly.

As we have seen, this position is one of the most difficult to pass through. If mistakes are going to be made they are most likely to be initiated in between the starting position and the area where the bar passes the knees. The lifter will be under pressure in two respects; firstly, there is mechanical disadvantage due to the existence of the weight-arm between the active fulcrum of the hips and the weight and, secondly, the great strength of the major muscle groups of the legs and hips lift the bar to knee height, but this is followed by a transfer from these muscles to those which will extend the hips and the back as the lifter moves into extension. It is inevitable that when such a change-over takes place, there will be a weak area to pass through. The second key position

is, therefore, the most important technical section of the lift.

A summary of this second key position is as follows.

1 **Feet**   The lifter is still balanced over all of his feet.
2 **Knees**   The legs, having driven against the inertia of the bar, will have lifted it to knee height. The knees will consequently be virtually straight, shins vertical, with the bar close to the knee-cap.
3 **Back**   The angle of the back will have been maintained from the starting position, being flat and in a strong position.
4 **Shoulders**   The shoulders are in advance of the bar.
5 **Arms**   The arms are straight, with the elbows still rotated out. This helps to keep the shoulders forwards and will ensure that the lift is upwards in the full extension.
6 **Head**   The head position remains the same.

This position is of vital importance for it is here that the lifter will feel maximum resistance due to the mechanical and anatomical reasons that have been explained. The lifter must be passing through this position correctly. The greatest possible emphasis must be placed upon this in coaching.

The clean: maximum upward extension; at this stage the lifter must force the hips up and in towards the bar

(3) Maximum upward extension

As the bar passes the knees and the lower part of the thighs, the lifter must force the hips up and in towards the bar. This will have the effect of steadily reducing the weight-arm and thereby placing the lifter in a more favourable position to exert maximum power at the top of the pull. It should be remembered that whilst this movement is the same as for the snatch, the problem is greater because the weight that is being lifted is much heavier. There will be a greater temptation to lean on the bar and the lifter must fight to 'stay over' as long as possible. In this way, the movement of the shoulders back and upwards will be as a reaction to the motion of the hip drive only. As the weight-arm is reduced, greater acceleration will be developed on the path of the bar. This will give momentum to the bar so that as the lifter moves from the position of maximum extension – dropping into the receiving position – the bar will continue to rise. This is very important for, when handling heavy weights, it must be remembered that the lifter will be unable to exert any lifting force as soon as the feet leave the platform.

As the lifter forces the hips up and into the bar he will start to come up onto the toes. The action of the muscles responsible for this and for the extension of the hip-joint will cause a slight re-bending of the knee. This is merely an anatomical accident and coaches who observe this phenomenon must recognise this and not try to coach it as part of the technique.

The clean: maximum upward extension; at the top of the pull the lifter will have achieved a position of lock at the major joint complexes

However, it is of value in the sense that it generates extra leg drive at the point of full extension which, in combination with a strong upward elevation of the shoulders towards the ears, will develop the momentum on the bar which is so vitally important.

At the top of the pull the lifter will have achieved a position of lock at the major joint complexes of ankle, knee and hip, with the shoulders over the bar in an upward pulling position. This full extension – with the shoulders elevated and the arms still straight – is the third key position. Lifters will be urged to 'Reach up', 'Finish the pull', 'Extend'; these phrases are used to encourage the lifter to achieve the position of maximum upward extension, thereby imparting maximum acceleration and height and, consequently, momentum that is so essential to a successful lift.

A summary of this third key position is as follows.

1 **Feet** The lifter drives high up onto the toes.
2 **Knees** The knees are now straight.
3 **Hips** The hips are up and into the bar.
4 **Arms** The arms now begin to bend with a strong elevation of the shoulders up to the ears. This is an upward shrug and not a pulling back of the shoulders.
5 **Head** The head drives up to the ceiling.

The lifter is seen to be in a fully extended position. By a correctly linked series of muscle group action, momentum will be imparted to the bar. This will ensure that the bar continues to rise when the lifter jumps his feet out, and to the side when he starts the drop.

(4) The receiving position

From the position of maximum upward extension, the lifter drops into the low sitting position to catch the bar on the chest. This action requires great speed and, as in the snatch, proficient lifters need to be some of the fastest moving athletes. To achieve this, the feet are jumped out and to the side and the knees are turned. This action allows the hips to be lowered between the heels whilst keeping the upper two-thirds of the trunk upright. There is, of course, a natural curve in the lumbar spine in the squat; the hips, as well as moving down, will also move slightly back from the position they were in at full extension. The lifter is coached to 'Sit in and sit up', meaning that the hips should be sat close to the heels and the chest held up. This gives a strong platform of support for the bar as it comes onto the chest.

The drop under the bar is accelerated by the lifter pulling vigorously on the bar as the feet leave the platform and it is an important consideration in coaching. This action of bending the arms also initiates the forward and upward movement of the elbows as the bar is brought onto the chest.

As has been explained, the trunk must be maintained upright as the lifter drops. Frequently, lifters dip their chests towards the bar in an effort to get under it fast. This causes them to 'fold up' and the bar can slip off the shoulders as they attempt to catch it. Achieving the upright extension of the trunk is difficult enough so it must be maintained as the lifter moves under the bar. Providing this has been done, the elbows should be raised and well clear from the knees and thighs. There are two very important reasons for this: firstly, should the elbows touch the knees or thighs during this part of the lift, the referees will disqualify the lifter for an 'elbow touch'; secondly, should the bar come down forwards heavily, all the weight will be taken on the arms, forcing the elbows down onto the knees with the very real possibility of serious injury to the wrists.

A summary of the receiving position is as follows.

1 **Feet** Jumped out to the side and placed firmly on the platform.

2 **Knees** Turned so that they point out in the same direction as the feet.

3 **Hips** Set slightly back in the sitting position, close between the heels. The lifter is coached to 'Sit in and sit up'.

4 **Back** Related to the position of the hips and the natural curve of the lumbar spine in the squatting position, the upper two-thirds of the trunk are vertical.

5 **Arms** As the lifter moves under the bar, the elbows will be brought up and high to secure the bar on the top of the chest and shoulders.

In the recovery from this deep squat receiving position, the lifter must keep the knees out and, when he stands erect, step the feet back into hip width position. Before he jerks the weight he may adjust the position of the bar on the top of the chest. It is frequently very important to make this adjustment because a heavy barbell pressing against the throat after a bad recovery may impair the breathing and cause the lifter to become giddy and eventually lose control of the bar.

**The clean:
receiving position**

Recovery from the low squat receiving position

Having cleaned the weight onto the chest, the lifter must now stand up and position himself for the jerk. This heavy front squat can take a lot out of the lifter; great leg power is essential so that the lifter will not be too exhausted before the jerk. To recover, the lifter tilts the trunk very slightly forwards, keeping the elbows high. This action will lift the buttocks, thereby opening the knee-joint slightly and relieving the great pressure of the full squat. This will help to start the recovery, giving those muscles which extend the knee-joint a better angle of pull. The lifter must force his way up, keeping the knees out. The muscles on the inside of the thigh – the adductors – are strong and there is a tendency for the knees to be pulled in as the legs are straightened. This action will force the hips back and the shoulders will dip forwards, making it more difficult to keep the bar on the chest. In all squatting exercises the lifter must always keep the knees out. Having stood erect, he steps his feet back into hip width position and settles himself prior to the jerk.

The jerk

Having recovered from the clean, the lifter steps the feet back into the hip width position. As has been described, the lifter will most certainly be feeling the effects of the clean and the recovery, especially when the weight is very heavy. He must take time to adjust his position and to allow himself to recover. However, by the same token, to stand with very heavy weights on the chest can, in itself, be very fatiguing. The most important point is to be able to breathe and, consequently, adjustment of the position of the bar should be made. This is permitted in the rules.

The key positions

(1) The starting position

The lifter must stand erect, well balanced over both of his feet. The chest must be held high with the bar resting on the tops of the anterior surface of the shoulders and chest. This position is helped by maintaining the forward position of the elbows, which keeps the bar high. The hips must be kept square to the front and directly under the body. Lifters are strongly advised to tighten the muscles of the hip and buttock in this position. This must be a very determined stance, with the chin tucked in so that there will be a clear path along which the bar can be driven, close past the face.

The jerk: starting position

41

(2) The dip

From the starting position, the lifter 'dips' or lowers the body. This movement must be performed with great control, so the inexperienced lifter is coached to dip slowly. As the lifter becomes more advanced and handles greater weights, so the dip technique can become crisper. This faster dip will enable the lifter to take advantage of the spring of the bar. However, very little spring on the bar will occur until the lifter handles weights in excess of 150 kg, so for many lifters, especially in the lighter classes, the more controlled approach is required.

The position of the body as described in the starting position must be maintained throughout the dip. The trunk must be upright, with the chest held high and the elbows up. This last described position of the elbows is very important as some lifters allow the elbows to drop when dipping. This causes the bar to roll off the top of the chest at precisely the moment when the lifter is starting to drive up, obviously causing problems. The bar must be kept on the shoulders, for it is from this stable platform that the impetus to the upward drive will begin.

The depth to which the lifter can dip whilst maintaining this upright position of the trunk will depend upon the flexibility of the ankle-joint (dorsi flexion), whilst maintaining the feet flat on the floor. Since this flexion is limited, the dip is shallow. This is not a disadvantage since the shorter range of movement of driving up from this position will be faster and more powerful. To relate this principle to boxing, it is often the shorter jab that will be much more powerful and effective than the long, swinging 'haymaker'. Should the lifter dip too low, however, he is likely to assume positions which will detrimentally affect the potential for an effective and powerful upward drive. Two major errors are as follows.

Whilst maintaining the feet flat on the floor, the lifter continues to dip down lower than the constraints of the ankle flexibility permit. He will not be able to maintain an upright trunk. The hips will move backwards and this action will incline the trunk forwards. This then sets a forward direction for the bar when the lifter starts to drive and it will end up in front of the

The jerk: the dip

lifter and will not be controllable in the arm-lock position. This is a common error, especially with the beginner.

Secondly, the lifter maintains an upright trunk whilst sinking down too low which forces him up onto his toes. This causes the knees to be thrust forwards and there is a serious forward loss of balance off the small base of the toes. This error is less likely to occur but either will reduce the possibility of a successful jerk. Remember that, as with all these movements, balance is of great importance if the lifter is to be able to exert maximum power.

A summary of the dip, the second key position, is as follows.

1 **Feet**   Flat on the floor.
2 **Trunk**   Upright throughout the dip. This position is dependent on the flexibility of the ankle-joint, whilst maintaining the trunk in an upright position.
3 **Arms**   Elbows held high, keeping the bar high onto the top of the shoulders. The lifter may make adjustments to this position after he has recovered from the clean. Do not drop the elbows during the dip.
4 **Chest**   Keep the chest up.
5 **Hips**   The hips must be set square to the front and tightened up prior to the commencement of the dip. This position must be kept throughout the movement.

The jerk: the drive

(3) The drive

It is important to remember that the dip is employed to initiate the drive upwards against the bar. This may seem obvious but there are always a number of lifters who dip and immediately split into the receiving position. This is incorrect and makes the jerk much more difficult to complete, since it throws all the resistance on the arms alone.

From the low position, the lifter must drive up against the bar. The upright position of the trunk is maintained and the elbows are kept up to secure the bar on the top of the chest and shoulders as he drives up onto the toes. This drive must be vertical and if the dip has been performed correctly, with an upright body position, there should be no difficulty. The drive must be very dynamic for it is necessary to overcome the inertia of the bar on the shoulders and start the upward movement of the bar. The drive will only take the bar to approximately mouth height, as it would be impossible to throw it to arms' length unless it was very light. With very heavy weights, in excess of 150 kg, the natural spring of the bar can assist with the drive. When the lifter dips, the bend in the bar will be downwards and as he starts to drive up, there will be an upward spring on the bar. This

action, in conjunction with the correct timing of the upward drive onto the toes, will accelerate the movement of the bar, giving upward momentum. Whilst this manoeuvre is of great help to the lifter, it must be remembered that deliberate bouncing of the bar on the shoulders is a cause for disqualification.

A summary of the drive is as follows.

1 **Feet**   Drive high up onto the toes.
2 **Trunk**   The trunk is upright throughout.
3 **Arms**   Keep the elbows up. In conjunction with the top of the drive, the arms begin to punch the bar above the head.
4 **Chest**   Keep the chest up.
5 **Hips**   Keep hips square and to the front.

The split

Having reached the top of the drive, the lifter must move into the receiving position with the weight above his head. Whilst a very few lifters punch the bar above the head and only dip the body to receive it above the head as in the power jerk, this tends to be rather unreliable and the recommended method of receiving the bar is on a high split. From this position – high on the toes, elbows up, driving the bar vertically from the chest – the lifter splits his feet fore and aft. This action will bring the lifter forwards under the bar. The lead for this movement is through the hips, which have been kept tight and in during the dip and drive. Both feet must move together from the platform.

There is only 15° of backward extension of the thigh-bone at the hip-joint; should the rear leg be kicked away too soon and too vigorously, the action will result in the trunk being tipped forwards and twisted to the side of the rear leg and the lifter will be in a poor position of support under the bar. Since this can be one of the major errors in performing the jerk, it bears repeating that the split must be even, with both feet leaving the platform together.

The key thought for the lifter is to 'Jerk high'. This means that the split receiving position must be high. If the lifter is pushed down or deliberately tries to drop low, the chances of recovery with heavy weights will be small. In the high receiving position, the angles of the legs will act as props up through the body, resisting the downward force of the weight. This action closely resembles that of buttresses on large buildings such as cathedrals, where the great weight of the rooves is supported through the walls, which are in turn buttressed.

The action of the arms will be to drive the bar upwards to the arm-lock position above the head. Again the emphasis is on driving and punching the bar high. The arms must be locked out in one movement. Any attempt to press the bar or any unlocking and re-locking of the arms is cause for disqualification, as is an uneven lock of one arm before the other. Referees will detect these faults, so this part of the action must be very positive.

The jerk: receiving position

(4) The receiving position

In the receiving position the lifter should be in a very strong position of support. The front leg will be bent at the knee with the thigh at approximately 45° to the horizontal. The front foot is flat on the ground. The rear leg has a slight bend at the knee; this will help the hips to come forwards. If the leg is stiff, the action will be to thrust and tip the body forwards with the hips being pulled back. The lifter is on the toe of the rear foot, which must be pointing fore and aft. On occasion, lifters turn the rear foot on the side. This incorrect action will twist the trunk away from the front and pull the hips back. The position of the hips is therefore square and to the front and under the body.

Adopt this position of the hips at the start of the dip and maintain it throughout the movement. In the receiving position, the bar, head, shoulders and hips should all be in a line of support, one directly beneath the other and the whole over the effective centre of the base between the front and the rear foot. This will be slightly towards the front foot, which takes a greater proportion of the resistance and through which any slight adjustment of balance can be made.

A summary of the receiving position is as follows.

1 **Feet**   The feet are jumped fore and aft in a short split. They skim across the platform. The front foot is flat and the rear foot is on the toes, with the heel pointing backwards.
2 **Trunk**   The hips have led the lifter forwards and under the bar so that the trunk is vertical, in a strong position of support.
3 **Arms**   The arms are rammed to lock above the head.
4 **Chest**   The chest is up.
5 **Hips**   The bar, shoulders, trunk and hips are all in a line of support over the effective centre of the base.

The recovery

The recovery from the split receiving position is very important – many attempts have been lost due to rushing the recovery. If the bar has been driven above the head correctly as has been described, the recovery should be performed with comparative ease. Problems occur if the bar has been directed forwards during the dip and the drive as this will set the recovery to the front and the lifter will be dragged off balance and will run to the front of the platform – the bar is frequently dropped under these circumstances. Any tendency to recover forwards off the rear foot can initiate these problems.

Recovery, therefore, must be off the front foot, moving it back a short step. The lifter must check his balance and then, with care, step the rear foot into line with the front foot. The lifter then remains standing motionless until the signal from the referee is given to replace the bar on the platform. The bar must be controlled as it is lowered and whilst it does not have to be brought back to the shoulders, it must not be dropped without the lifter retaining a grip on it throughout its descent.

Teaching the jerk

As has already been stated, the jerk is a very difficult phase of the whole movement – the lifter is under great pressure, following the clean, with his energy draining away quickly. It is therefore essential that the technique of the movement is as accurate as possible.

Since the basic receiving position for the jerk is dependent on correct placement of the hips under the body, it is essential that there is sufficient extensibility at the hip-joint of the rear leg. This is approximately 15° and this range must be utilised to the full. In the days when split technique was prevalent, achieving this mobility did not present a problem because the full lunging position was involved in every snatch and clean. Generally the jerk was performed correctly. With the change to the squat technique of snatching and cleaning, however, this repeated extensibility of the hip-joint was lost because the more modern method is to flex the hip and place the chest forwards in the receiving positions of the squat lifts.

In moving under the bar, there is a tendency to repeat this action of pushing the chest forwards with the hips moving back. This is further exaggerated by the lack of mobility in extension of the hip-joint and the lifter receives the bar in the 'squatter's jerk' position – chest pushed forwards, head poking through the line of the bar, hips back and the thigh of the rear leg in a vertical position. This is a weak receiving stance, with the forces of support being out of line and with no common resultant resistance

being achieved. In addition, the lifter is frequently forced to recover forwards, with a subsequent loss of balance due to the forward thrust of the chest.

Considering the problem of the squatter's jerk, it may well be advisable to coach the jerk before any other lifting movement. In this way the young lifter will develop the mobility in the hip-joint before it is adversely affected by squatting techniques. The best method of achieving this is through the jerk balance exercise (see page 57). This exercise will teach the lifter how to move under the bar, with the hips square to the front and with the body in an upright position. It can be followed with full jerking, taking the weight from stands, as the lifter becomes fully mobile and learns the correct position of support under the bar – shoulders, trunk and hips all in line over the effective centre of the base.

Since the initial concept of weight lifting for all beginners is to lift the bar above the head, this exercise will go a long way to fulfilling their view of the sport and will be easier to perform than the snatch, which is most generally taught first. In addition to this exercise, the lifter should warm up with full range free-standing lunging movements in order to develop the full extensibility of the hip-joint of the rear leg.

The teaching objectives of this approach are as follows.

1 To give the essential feel of lifting weights above the head. This encourages and develops enthusiasm for lifting.
2 To develop a keen sense of balance with the weight above the head in a high receiving position.
3 To develop mobility of the hip-joint so that the lifter can be placed correctly under the bar in the most effective position of support.
4 To develop confidence with weights above the head.
5 To develop arm and shoulder strength.

Whilst many coaches will consider that the complexity of the snatch requires all their attention in the early stages, the above approach may be beneficial in the long run and ensure that problems with the jerk will be minimised. Remember, it is often strength in the jerk that finally wins the contest.

THE DOUBLE KNEE BEND PHENOMENON

The action of leaning against the weight causes the lifter to jump away from the bar and, in addition, transfers the effort to directing the barbell backwards. It becomes impossible to control the path of a heavy barbell under these circumstances. This is a cardinal mistake in weight lifting but is understandable in that the lifter, in endeavouring to overcome the resistance, uses his bodyweight in the same way as a participant in a tug-of-war leans back against the rope. In addition, full extension is prevented and the reaction is for the feet to jump forwards as the shoulders go backwards.

Since these errors result from moving the fulcrum of the shoulders backwards to the vertical line through the weight, then it must be the hip-joint which is to be moved. The hip-joint, therefore, becomes the active fulcrum and must be driven in and upwards towards the weight. This action reduces the weight-arm, develops acceleration on the upward path of the barbell, and allows those muscles which extend the body into the upright pulling position to work at their maximum efficiency.

In watching the lifter performing this movement, it will be observed that the shoulders do, in effect, move backwards. This movement, however, is a reaction to the forward motion of the hip-joint. Nevertheless, the lifter is still coached to try to keep his shoulders forwards as long as possible so that at the top of the pull, he is in an upright lifting position over the bar.

During these first two stages of the lift, the knees will be seen almost to straighten and then to re-bend as the hips are driven in. This is an anatomical accident and is not a coachable technique. However, confusion in analysing the mechanics and anatomy involved has led to serious coaching errors. This phenomenon – known as the 'double knee bend' – is seen to occur during a phase of the pull between the second and third key positions. If the barbell has been lifted from the floor correctly, utilising the major muscles of the legs, it will be seen that when it reaches the second key position at knee height, the legs at the knee-joint are virtually straight with the lifter flat on his feet, having maintained the angle of the back.

From this position the lifter must endeavour to achieve a position of maximum upward extension. This requires that the active fulcrum of the hips be driven in and upwards, towards the vertical line through the barbell. At the same time as the lifter achieves this final position, he will be rising up on his toes. It is during this phase of the movement that the knees bend and move forwards for a second time. Ultimately, this second bending of the knees will be of advantage to the lifter as it gives him an extra 'kick' upwards, thereby providing extra acceleration to the barbell at the top of the pull. Since this is seen to be advantageous, a deliberate bending and pushing forwards of the knees is often coached. The real action, however, is an anatomical accident.

Study of simple anatomy and kinetics of this stage of the movement will show that those muscles which extend the hip-joint also flex the knee, and the muscle which helps the lifter to rise up on his toes in a load-bearing position also flexes the knee. This strong action at the hip and ankle-joint causes knee bending and whilst it is advantageous to the lifter, it is accidental. Here is an anatomical analysis of this action.

Extension of the hip and flexion of the knee
Muscles in action: (1) *Biceps femoris* (long head), from tuberosity of the ischium (base of the pelvis) to the lateral head of the tibia and

fibula. (2) *Semi tendinosus*, from tuberosity of the ischium to the upper part of the inner surface of the tibia. (3) *Semi membranosus*, from tuberosity of the ischium to the posterior surface of the back of the head of the tibia. This group of muscles is commonly referred to as the 'hamstring group' and comes strongly into play in all lifting movement.

**Extension of the ankle-joint
and flexion of the knee**
Muscle in action: *Gastrocnemius*, from heel-bone via the Achilles tendon to the posterior aspect of the femur (back of the knee-joint). This muscle is a prime mover for plantar flexion of the ankle-joint when in a load-bearing position. It is a true flexor of the knee-joint.

Mistaken coaching of a deliberate second knee bend will result in the following.

1   The lifter comes forwards on his toes too soon.
2   The knees, being bent far too early, are pushed forwards. These two errors together result in loss of balance.
3   There is a lowering of the body with a consequent diminishing of upward lifting force on the barbell and also an exaggerated forward displacement of the bar.

THE TECHNIQUE OF THE SPLIT

The split

It is very rare now that split technique is used in lifting. Those lifters who do so either have come from some other sport – such as athletics – comparatively late in their training, or who are older and have mobility problems in the squat receiving positions.

All lifters who practise the split technique must pay great attention to maintaining their position on two feet for as long as possible in the full extension of the pull. This is a beautiful technique but is not quite as efficient in the full development of maximum power as the squat-style lifts. For this reason it has ceased to be an effective technique in modern weight lifting. All sections of the 'pick up' part of the lift are very similar to those for the squat style.

The two hands snatch

During the final drive into extension at the top of the pull, the split lifter must pay particular attention to driving the hips in and up towards the bar. This action will take the lifter down and forwards once the feet leave the ground. From the position of maximum upward extension, the lifter comes off both feet at exactly the same time to split them fore and aft. It is essential that all those who employ this technique are coached to come off both feet together. Having said this, it is only fair to point out that in detailed study of all the great split lifters, the rear foot has always moved fractionally before the front foot. This is due to the following facts.

1   There is only some 15° of backward extension at the hip-joint.
2   However hard we try for a direct upward extension, there is inevitably some slight lean back with maximum weights which causes the

lifter to move the rear foot in order to be in a position to re-establish his balance.

3   The rear leg travels further and, consequently, needs to move faster.

At the highest level of lifting these phenomena will be basically subconscious and, as already explained, a very definite attempt must be made to ensure that the rear foot leaves the ground at the same time as the front foot. Lifters of a more limited standard are often seen to move the rear foot well before the completion of the extension. The results of this error are various.

1   The lifter is left pulling on one leg only and is, consequently, badly out of balance.

2   He can only exert force through the one leg (front) as that is the only part of the body in contact with the ground.

3   Because of the limited extension at the hip-joint, the body can be tilted forwards by throwing a leg back vigorously.

4   Any attempt at a hip swing in and upwards, towards the bar, will be killed. In fact, the hips can only be pulled back and twisted away from the line of the barbell.

All these aspects combine to diminish seriously the lifter's ability to use his full power potential. For these reasons the split technique is now rarely used. However, some people – especially if they come to weight lifting a little later in their lives – may find that problems of flexibility, particularly in the upper spine, will make satisfactory performance of the squat technique difficult; but it will still be possible for them to achieve first-class results using split technique, providing they pay very careful attention to detail and receive good quality coaching.

Assuming that the lifter has chosen to perform the split technique, let us consider the further technical requirements. Having reached maximum upward extension, the lifter comes off both feet together. The inward and upward action of the hips will now take the lifter forwards as he drops down underneath the barbell. It is essential that he maintains the upright position of the trunk, allowing the hips to lead him under the bar. No attempt should be made to push the head and shoulders forwards – such a movement is quite unnecessary. The feet will come to land at approximately the same time, although the rear foot may touch down fractionally before the front. The forward action of the hips will allow them to travel down and towards the front heel, and the knee will travel forwards in advance of the ankle. The receiving position is very low. One of the reasons for disqualification is when the knee of the rear leg touches the platform. If the hip drive forwards and upwards has been allowed to continue, there should be no danger of this occurring because the direction of force will be out over the front ankle and the forward knee.

The action of the arms in moving under the bar is slightly different from that employed by the squat technique lifter. As the lifter is moving forwards, he is rotating the bar within its own axis and as the body comes beneath it, he must punch out vigorously with the heels of the hands. The balance in this receiving position is critical – displacement of the lifter or the barbell from side to side causes serious problems of control. Of the two techniques, this is probably the more gymnastic and gives great satisfaction in correct performance.

To recover from this low position, the lifter must tilt the barbell carefully backwards. This action will relieve pressure on the tightly compressed front knee-joint; at the same time, stiffening the rear leg, he should push strongly with the front and step it in a short pace. By tilting the bar very slightly forwards, the rear leg can then be brought into line with the front foot. Recovery in this way is important. Should the rear foot be moved before the front one, there is a tendency for the body to incline forwards and for the lifter to begin to run towards the front of the platform. Many an otherwise successful lift has been lost because of faulty recovery.

The techniques of weight lifting are very difficult to master and the more often you are confronted with the essential basic elements, the more likely you are to perform the movements correctly and achieve satisfactory results. The weight lifter must be a thinking athlete, concerned at all times with developing technique. A summary of the crucial points of the two hands snatch using the split technique is as follows.

1 Feet Split fore and aft, front foot flat on the floor with toe turned slightly inwards. Rear foot on the ball of the foot with heel straight so that whole foot is directed to front.
2 Knees Front knee is bent and pushed forwards over the front foot. Rear leg has very slight flexion at the knee-joint but is strongly supportive.
3 Hips Square to the front and close towards the front heel.
4 Trunk Maintained upright. Arms are locked and pushing vigorously against the barbell above the head.

The clean

With regard to the clean, the squat technique is taught in most instances; but heavy weights can still be lifted employing the split technique. However, the problems inherent in this style, outlined earlier, restrict the lifter from achieving the best possible results.

Having reached the position of maximum upward extension, the lifter must come off both feet together. The hip action will ensure that he drops down and forwards underneath the bar. He should pull vigorously on the barbell as his feet leave the floor, but must ensure that he maintains the angle of the trunk, which will have a slight backward incline, due to the forward emphasis of the hip movement as he drops under the bar.

Both feet will land at approximately the same time. The rear foot should be pointing directly fore and aft and the front foot will have turned slightly inwards, with the knee travelling forwards and pushed well forwards over the ankle-joint in the same direction. The hips (which must be maintained square to the front) will be close to the forward heel. Because of the slight backward inclination of the trunk, the barbell can be secured upon the chest without such a high elbow action as is required in the squat technique.

This receiving position requires great sense of balance and, when performed correctly, is undoubtedly one of the most satisfying and beautiful movements in weight lifting.

To recover from this low receiving position, the rear leg is stiffened and is used as a rotating prop, pivoting on the rear toe. The bar will be tipped slightly backwards, thereby helping to relieve pressure on the forward knee, which should be vigorously extended in combination with these two movements. As the front leg nears complete extension, the foot is stepped back a few inches. The lifter now pushes off the rear leg (which continues to raise the body and bring the weight forwards and upwards), stepping the rear foot into line with the front one to complete this section of the movement, prior to the jerk.

Before jerking the weight from the shoulders, the lifter may make adjustments of the bar at the neck. This is sometimes necessary as the heavy barbell presses against the throat and after a hard recovery from the receiving position, it is essential that the lifter breathes freely.

A summary of the clean using the split technique is as follows.

1 Feet Split fore and aft, front foot flat on floor with toe turned slightly inwards. Rear foot on ball of foot with heels straight so that the foot is directed to the front.
2 Knees Front knee is bent and pushed forwards over the front foot. Rear leg has very slight flexion at the knee-joint.
3 Hips Square to the front and close towards front heel.
4 Trunk Inclined slightly backwards due to forward action of the hip-joint.
5 Arms Because the trunk is inclined slightly backwards, a high elbow action is not necessary. But the arms are so placed as to secure the bar on top of the chest.

ASSISTANCE EXERCISES

The two hands snatch

Power snatch

The bar is lifted from the floor to above the head on straight arms, with only the slightest bending of the knees. The feet should not be moved. As is clear from the name of this exercise, its objective is to develop power in those muscles employed in the snatch. Its special value is in compelling the lifter to maintain a long pull.

The power snatch can also be performed from various heights as in snatching from the hang – where the bar is held at levels in the knee region – and from blocks of varying height. When the lifter executes these movements, either from the hang or from blocks, it is essential that he is coached most carefully because there is a tendency on the part of the lifter to try to start the motion by throwing the head and shoulders backwards. This must be counteracted.

Snatch pulls with full body extension

Here, the first phase of the snatching movement – lifting the bar from the floor to a position of full extension – is completed. This exercise can be performed with weights in the following two ranges.

1 Snatch pulls to 100% This means that weights up to the equivalent of the lifter's best performance in the two hands snatch are used. At this range, the exercise is highly dynamic.

2 Snatch pulls to maximum This means that weights are handled that are well above the lifter's snatching ability, but that permit the lifter to go through manoeuvres which are still essentially those that would be followed in performing the complete lift. It is essential that loss of technique is prevented. These movements are not dead lifts.

In all types of snatch pulls, deliberate attempts to bend the arms, as in an upright rowing movement, must be avoided. The lifter must concentrate on strong elevation of the shoulders. Any arm movement is rather as a result of momentum imparted to the bar by the correct build-up of force. Pulling manoeuvres for the snatch can be executed from the hang or from blocks but, once again, it is vital that very careful coaching is provided for the lifter carrying out these movements.

Snatch width grip shrugs

This exercise is designed to develop the ability of the lifter to elevate his shoulders strongly at the conclusion of the full extension. It must not be confused with the shoulder rolling movement of bodybuilders. The lifter should use straps because the weight must be very heavy.

With a snatch width grip, the lifter stands erect with the bar resting across the front of the thighs. Keeping the trunk erect and the feet flat on the floor, he bends his knees and then drives vigorously upwards onto his toes, at the same time pulling the shoulders up to the ears. The arms should not bend during the movement. Inclining the trunk forwards during the dip is not recommended because it tends to cause the lifter to pull the shoulders back against the resistance.

Left **Snatch pull with full body extension**

Halting dead lift

This exercise is similar to snatching from the hang, but the position with the bar at knee height is maintained for a period of approximately six seconds. This places considerable resistance upon the muscles which are employed in the middle range of the movement; these muscles are working isometrically.

At the conclusion of the six-second period, the lifter completes the movement by reaching up to full extension. The bar is then lowered to the starting position at knee height and the procedure is repeated. It is not necessary to perform many repetitions of this manoeuvre because the overload is so great.

The clean

Power clean

The bar is lifted from the floor onto the top of the chest with only the slightest bending of the knees as the bar is received. It is important to remember that the feet must not be moved

Power clean

from the starting position. There is a tendency with heavy weights to attempt to jump the feet out to the side. This defeats the object of the exercise – to sustain the pulling motion for as long as possible, thereby developing the muscles responsible for this movement. The lifter must therefore endeavour to maintain as long, and as high, a pull as possible, keeping his feet in the starting position.

This exercise can be performed from blocks of various height, but it is important that it is coached carefully to avoid any tendency to try to start the movement by leading with the head and shoulders backwards.

53

Clean pulls with full body extension

This exercise is designed to develop pulling power up to the position of full extension of the body. It is performed with weights in the following two categories.

1   **Clean pulls to 100%**   Here, weights in the range of the lifter's best performance of the two hands clean and jerk are used. The exercise is dynamic and the lifter must concentrate on developing speed within the technical range.
2   **Clean pulls to maximum**   In these movements, the lifter can handle very heavy weights which are above his normal cleaning ability. But it must be remembered that correct technique must be maintained in executing these assistance exercises as they are a vital part of the complete movement. These movements are not dead lifts.

In all pulling manoeuvres for the clean, deliberate attempts to bend the arms must be avoided. Any arm action of this nature would prevent correct force being applied to the bar. At the top of the movement, the lifter must concentrate on strong elevation of the shoulders. Again, these pulling manoeuvres can be executed from the hang or from blocks. Since the weight is considerable, great care must be taken in coaching to ensure that correct technical pathways are maintained.

Clean grip shrugs

This exercise throws great resistance upon those muscles which elevate the shoulders and is, therefore, most important in the development of a full and effective extension. Do not confuse this manoeuvre with shoulder rolling, performed by bodybuilders.

Using straps and a clean width grip, the lifter stands erect, allowing the bar to rest across the front of the thighs. Maintaining his trunk erect and his feet flat on the floor, he bends his knees and drives vigorously upwards onto his toes, at the same time pulling the shoulders up towards the ears.

As this exercise is specific to the muscles which elevate the shoulders, the arms must not be bent during the movement. Be careful not to

Clean pull with full body extension

allow the body to incline forwards to any great degree at the start of the manoeuvre because there is a danger that the lifter may try to pull backwards with his shoulders in order to overcome the inertia of the heavy resistance. Remember to drive up strongly.

Halting dead lift

This is the same movement as is performed in the snatch manoeuvre on page 52, but now we employ the shoulder width grip. Careful coaching is essential.

Whilst all of these exercises listed above will have very definite beneficial effects upon the strength development of the muscles of the legs and hips, there are an additional two specialised leg exercises, depending upon the type of technique employed, which aid the recovery from the low receiving position in either split or squat. These are known as front and split squats.

Front squats

The lifter takes the bar onto the front of the chest, the bar being held in position at the shoulders by the hands. The elbows must be kept up, the feet placed wider than hip width apart with the toes turned out. The lifter now lowers into the deep squat position and from there recovers. This movement is repeated a specified number of times.

Above and over **Front squat**

It is essential that the lifter maintains an upright position, with the elbows held up throughout the movement. The knees must be kept turned out and apart during the recovery, fighting against the tendency for the adductor muscles on the inside of the leg to pull the knees in.

The feet should be placed in the same position in which they will land during the actual clean. This means that the lifter should perform a squat clean and the location of his feet, when he receives the bar, should then be marked on the platform. It is a good idea to make a permanent indication of this foot spacing in front of the squat stands. The lifter may then step back and place his feet on these marks to perform the exercise.

Split squat

Split squats

The lifter takes the bar from the stands on his chest and steps forwards on a predetermined foot spacing and from this lowers the body down and forwards into the complete split clean receiving position. From here, by stiffening the rear leg, he pushes backwards with the front one and then repeats the movement up and down.

This exercise develops great power and mobility in the receiving position and generates great confidence. Do not attempt repetitions of this exercise until you are perfectly balanced. It should be pointed out that strength development is very specific in this manoeuvre. Often lifters who can produce very good results on the normal back squat will still find it difficult in this movement and will be surprised at the initial low weight with which they will struggle.

This is a very useful exercise for the beginner to practise in mobilising the front of the hip-joint. This essential hip-joint extensibility will have great beneficial effect on the receiving position in the jerk.

Jerk balance

The jerk

Jerk balance

This exercise is valuable both in teaching the jerk from the shoulders to the beginner and for developing power in the receiving position and re-establishing technique for the more advanced lifter.

The lifter takes the bar from the stands and, taking a very short step forwards, assumes the starting position in which weight is evenly distributed over both feet, with the trunk nearly vertical. The bar must be resting solidly on the chest and the toe of the rear foot must be pointing directly fore and aft, with the hips set square to the front. From this position, the lifter bends both knees quickly and, driving up vigorously, punches the bar above the head with the arms. At the same time, the front foot is stepped very slightly forwards and the body is dipped by bending the knee as the bar is received above the head. The lifter then lowers the bar and recovers back to the starting position, withdrawing the front foot slightly.

Jerk from behind neck

This exercise follows the normal jerking procedure except that the starting position is with the weight on top of the shoulders, at the back of the neck.

Jerk from behind neck

Heave jerks

This manoeuvre is a very valuable power builder. The lifter drives the bar from the chest above the head to arms' length, dipping at the knees and hips to catch the weight. There is no foot movement in this exercise.

Above, right and below **Heave jerk**

Quarter jerks

This exercise is designed specifically to develop power in driving the bar from the chest. It is often performed in racks, where very heavy weights can be handled.

From the position of the bar resting on the chest, the lifter bends the legs and drives up vigorously onto the toes against the resistance. With maximum weights the bar may hardly leave the chest at the top of the drive.

These exercises are technical and can be valuable in the learning process. At the same time, they become very important power developers for the more advanced lifters. Listed below are other exercises which, whilst being technical in some respects, are generally considered to be more valuable as basic raw power developers.

Quarter jerk

Above, right and below **Back squat**

Back squats

The back squat is an essential movement in all forms of weight lifting and very considerable resistance can be handled. Weights should be taken from squat stands onto the shoulders, behind the lifter's head. From this position, he lowers into the full squat position, driving up vigorously in recovery.

Squat jumps

This exercise is particularly beneficial in the concluding phase of all upward driving movements. The barbell rests across the lifter's shoulders, behind his head, and from there he lowers to a shallow squat and, driving high, leaps into the air. In landing, the knees are bent to act as shock absorbers. It is important to remember that the lifter must check between each repetition because continuous leaping up and down can damage knee-joints.

Leg press

This requires the use of the leg-press machine in which the lifter assumes a position underneath the resistance which is very similar to the starting position were he to be turned onto his feet. The legs are straightened strongly against the resistance. This develops great power in the first stage of the pull.

Calf raises

This exercise is specifically geared to those muscles which assist the lifter to complete the pull by lifting him onto his toes. The exercise is best performed in a special calf-raising machine.

Pressing movements

There is a variety of pressing exercises and a selection from these is essential to the necessary development of arm and shoulder strength. These movements are as follows: military press, seated press, seated inclined press (these movements can be performed using either a barbell or dumb-bells), press behind neck and bench press.

For the Olympic lifter, bench pressing is regarded as the recuperative exercise to be executed at the end of a schedule, to help stimulate relaxed breathing. Very heavy weights should not be used because this tightens up the muscles on the front of the chest and shoulders, restricting mobility and thereby making it more difficult for the lifter to hold his arms directly above his head.

Seated press

Above and above right **Seated press behind neck**

Above and above right **Seated press with dumb-bells**

'Good morning' exercise

This is best performed using a round back technique and is a very important rehabilitative and protective exercise. Lifters are taught correctly to maintain a flat back throughout all lifting movements. Should the resistance, however, be so great that they are pulled strongly into a position where the spine rounds, it is possible for some minor injury to occur to the intrinsic muscles which lie along the spine. The round back 'Good morning' exercise is performed to counteract this possible danger.

With the bar resting across the back of the neck, feet hip width apart, the lifter unlocks his knees slightly, bends the body forwards, allowing the spine to curl as he lowers down. He then assumes the upright stance position, straightening out the back from this curved state as he stands erect. As a result, the muscles which surround the spine are being exercised over their full range of movement. The exercise can be executed with a flat back also.

There are a number of general weight-training exercises which can be of benefit to the Olympic lifter. These generally deal with specific muscle groups and may be employed should there be any weakness within one of these groups.

Throughout this section, we have spoken of the use of straps. In the early stages, lifters should carry out movements without the use of this aid in order that their gripping ability can be developed.

Some of the pulling manoeuvres may be performed with the lifter standing on blocks. This is of particular benefit in the development of the initial stages of the pull because the lifter must lower the bar down beyond the normal starting position. Those muscles responsible for the start of the lift are compelled to work over a longer range. Generally, this exercise may be executed by lifters of advanced qualification only.

Upward jumps with a barbell or dumb-bells will benefit the driving potential of the lifter throughout the pulling movement. The nature of these types of exercise is very explosive.

Isometric pulls in racks

Here, the lifter exerts maximum force for short periods of time against a bar which may be fixed at any height within racks. The grip may vary from snatch to clean width. These exercises have value in developing muscle groups which may have weaknesses in some areas of their movement.

'Good morning' exercise

Pull to arms' length with dumb-bells

Pulls to arms' length with dumb-bells

This is similar to the power snatch manoeuvre, but heavy dumb-bells are used rather than a barbell. It requires very much greater control and all-round arm and shoulder power.

Power cleans with dumb-bells

This manoeuvre is similar to the power clean exercise, but using dumb-bells.

Supporting heavy weights above the head

Lifters are advised to perform this exercise in racks, where safety precautions can be taken. This exercise is very valuable in developing great determination and courage under the heaviest resistance.

Power clean with dumb-bells

Jerk with dumb-bells

Using dumb-bells rather than a barbell, this exercise is otherwise identical to the normal jerk.

Heave jerk with dumb-bells

Identical to the orthodox heave jerk, but using dumb-bells.

Summary of power assistance exercises

	Technical	Raw
Snatch	1 Power snatch 2 Snatch balance 3 Snatch grip pulls 100% 4 Snatch grip pull maximum 5 Snatch grip shrugs 6 Snatch from blocks 7 Halting dead lift	1 Power snatch without dip 2 Isometric pull in racks 3 Pull to arms' length with dumb-bells 4 Supporting heavy weights above head
Clean	1 Power clean 2 Clean grip pulls 100% 3 Clean grip pull maximum 4 Clean grip shrugs 5 Pulls from blocks 6 Halting dead lift 7 Split squats 8 Front squats	1 Power clean without dip 2 Power clean with dumb-bells 3 Isometric pull in racks
Jerk	1 Jerk balance 2 Jerk from behind neck 3 Jerk from racks 4 Heave jerks 5 Quarter jerks	1 Jerks with dumb-bells 2 Heave jerks with dumb-bells 3 Supporting heavy weights above head
General	Short range power movements for pulls	1 Back squats 2 Squat jumps 3 Calf raises 4 Press: military, seated, inclined 5 Round back 'Good morning' 6 Selected muscle group bodybuilding exercises 7 Grip development 8 Bench press

General assistance exercises

The training of a weight lifter is not confined to the use of weights alone. We must consider movements which will assist in the development of speed, flexibility, general cardio-vascular and circulo-respiratory endurance and activities often associated with other sports which will help to develop co-ordination, balance and dexterity and general awareness of the movement capabilities of the human body.

Exercises for cardio-vascular and circulo-respiratory endurance

General fitness exercises are very important to the weight lifter. The overload on the systems in performing the snatch, for example, is not very great because the duration of the movement is very short; however, it is essential that the lifter has a high level of recovery from one training schedule to the next. Since training programmes are progressive, the lifter must have the ability to recover quickly from one bout of heavy work to another.

This type of fitness is developed through running, climbing and swimming activities which last for a considerable length of time. This is achieved by extending the work-outs, increasing the number of repetitions in each set and various forms of circuit training.

Exercises for co-ordination, balance and dexterity

Many of the technical assistance exercises will help with the development of these qualities. In addition, participation in other sports and games – especially gymnastics and volleyball – will generate particular benefits. Remember that care must be taken in playing volleyball, basketball and handball to prevent damage to the fingers or thumbs.

Exercises for mobility

It is important to note that ballistic movements against the joint do not produce mobility; on the contrary, they add to the problems of lack of flexibility about the joint being exercised. There is a variety of simple movements which may be performed and the exerciser should relate these to all the major joint complexes, especially ensuring that he is flexible enough to achieve the lowest receiving positions. Those exercises with weights – such as the snatch balance movements – will assist greatly this essential aspect of a lifter's make-up.

Trunk rotation

Side bends will help to develop a full range of lateral flexion

Left **Arm circling will aid the mobility of the shoulder girdle**

Stretching the hamstring muscle group

Exercises for speed

1 Performance of power assistance exercises with very light barbells, at maximum speed.
2 Sprinting over short distances.
3 Standing long, high and triple jump.
4 Bounding and leaping movements.
5 Hurdling.
6 Hopping.
7 Shuttle running.
8 Shadow boxing and skipping.

Abdominal raises

Chest raises will strengthen the muscles of the back

INTERNATIONAL RULES

The two hands snatch

The rules below are taken verbatim from the handbooks of B.A.W.L.A. and I.W.L.F.

The barbell shall be placed horizontally in front of the lifter's legs. It shall be gripped, palms downwards, and pulled in a single movement from the ground to the full extent of both arms above the head, while either 'splitting' or bending the legs. The bar shall pass with a continuous movement along the body, of which no part other than the feet may touch the ground during the execution of the lift. The weight which has been lifted must be maintained in the final motionless position – arms and legs extended, feet on the same line – until the referee's signal to replace the bar on the platform. The turning over of the wrists must not take place until the bar has passed the top of the lifter's head. The lifter may recover in his own time, either from a 'split' or a 'squat'.

The referee's signal shall be given as soon as the lifter becomes absolutely motionless in all parts of the body and has his feet and barbell in line and parallel to the plane of the trunk.

Incorrect movements

1   Pulling from the hang.
2   Pause during the lifting of the bar.
3   Uneven extension of the arms.
4   Incomplete extension of the arms.
5   Finishing with a 'press-out'.
6   Bending and extending the arms during the recovery.
7   Touching the ground with the knee or buttocks or any part of the body other than the feet.
8   Leaving the platform during the execution of the lift, i.e. if touching – with any part of a foot – the floor outside the limits of the platform.
9   Replacing the bar on the platform before the referee's signal.
10   Dropping the bar after the referee's signal to replace it.
11   Failing to finish with the feet and the barbell in line and parallel to the plane of the trunk.

The clean and jerk

1st part: the clean

The bar shall be placed horizontally in front of the lifter's legs. It shall be gripped, palms downwards, and brought in a single movement from the ground to the shoulders, while either 'splitting' or bending the legs. The bar must not touch the chest before the final position. It shall then rest on the clavicles, or on the chest above the nipples, or on the fully bent arms. The feet shall be returned to the same line, legs straight, before performing the jerk. The lifter may make this recovery in his own time.

2nd part: the jerk

Bend the legs and extend them, as well as the arms, so as to bring the bar to the full stretch of the arms, vertically extended. Return the feet to the same line, arms and legs extended, awaiting the referee's signal to replace the bar on the platform. The referee's signal shall be given as soon as the lifter becomes absolutely motionless in all parts of the body and has his feet and the barbell on the same line, parallel to the plane of his trunk.

Important – after the clean and before the jerk, the lifter may assure the position of the bar. This must not lead to confusion. It cannot mean – in any case – granting a second movement to the lifter. But the lifter does have the following three options.

1   To withdraw his thumbs or to 'unhook' if he has used this method.
2   To lower the bar in order to rest it on his shoulders if it is placed too high and impeded his breathing or causes pain.
3   To change the width of his grip.

Incorrect movements – clean

1   Any unfinished attempt at pulling in which the bar has reached at least knee height.
2   Pulling from the hang.
3   Cleaning in two or more movements.
4   Touching the ground with the knee or buttocks or any part of the body other than the feet.
5   Any clean in which the bar touches a part of the trunk before the final position at the shoulders.
6   Cleaning in the squat position, touching the knees or thighs with the elbows or arms.
7   Leaving the platform during the execution of the lift, i.e. touching – with any part of the foot – the floor outside the limits of the platform.

Incorrect movements – jerk

8   Any apparent effort of jerking which is not completed.
9   Uneven extension of the arms.
10   Pause during the extension of the arms and finishing with a 'press-out'.
11   Bending and extending the arms during the recovery.
12   Leaving the platform during the execution of the lift, i.e. touching – with any part of a foot – the floor outside the limits of the platform.
13   Replacing the bar on the platform before the referee's signal.
14   Dropping the bar after the referee's signal to replace it.
15   Failing to finish with the feet and the barbell in line and parallel to the plane of the trunk.

PERCENTAGE TABLE

The figures below must be rounded up or down to the nearest 2.5 kg or 5 kg. For example, 85% of 122.5 kg is shown as 104.1 kg; round this up to 105 kg. Again 90% of 167.5 kg is shown as 150.7 kg; round this down to 150 kg.

kg	60%	65%	70%	75%	80%	85%	90%	92.5%	95%	97.5%	102.5%	105%	107.5%	110%
75	45	48.7	52.5	56.2	60	63.7	67.5	69.3	71.2	73.1	76.8	78.7	80.6	82.5
77.5	46.5	50.3	54.2	58.1	62	65.8	69.7	71.6	73.6	75.5	79.4	81.3	83.3	85.2
80	48	52	56	60	64	68	72	74	76	78	82	84	86	88
82.5	49.5	53.6	57.7	61.8	66	70.1	74.2	76.3	78.3	80.4	84.5	86.6	88.6	90.7
85	51	55.2	59.5	63.7	68	72.2	76.5	78.6	80.7	82.8	87.1	89.2	91.3	93.5
87.5	52.5	56.8	61.2	65.6	70	74.3	78.7	80.9	83.1	85.3	89.6	91.8	94	96.2
90	54	58.5	63	67.5	72	76.5	81	83.2	85.5	87.7	92.2	94.5	96.7	99
92.5	55.5	60.1	64.7	69.3	74	78.6	83.2	85.5	87.8	90.1	94.8	97.1	99.4	101.7
95	57	61.7	66.5	71.2	76	80.7	85.5	87.8	90.2	92.6	97.3	99.7	102	104.4
97.5	58.5	63.3	68.2	73.1	78	82.9	87.7	90.1	92.6	95	99.9	102.3	104.8	107.2
100	60	65	70	75	80	85	90	92.5	95	97.5	102.5	105	107.5	110
102.5	61.5	66.6	71.7	76.8	82	87.1	92.2	94.8	97.3	99.9	105	107.6	110.1	112.7
105	63	68.2	73.5	78.7	84	89.2	94.5	97.1	99.7	102.3	107.6	110.2	112.8	115.5
107.5	64.5	69.8	75.2	80.6	86	91.3	96.7	99.4	102.1	104.8	110.1	112.8	115.5	118.2
110	66	71.5	77	82.5	88	93.5	99	101.7	104.5	107.2	112.7	115.5	118.2	121
112.5	67.5	73.1	78.1	84.3	90	95.6	101.2	104	106.8	109.6	115.3	118.1	120.9	123.7
115	69	74.7	80.5	86.2	92	97.7	103.5	106.3	109.2	112.1	117.8	120.7	123.6	126.5
117.5	70.5	76.3	82.2	88.1	94	99.8	105.7	108.6	111.6	114.5	120.4	123.3	126.3	129.2
120	72	78	84	90	96	102	108	110.9	114	117	123	126	129	132
122.5	73.5	79.6	85.7	91.8	98	104.1	110.2	113.3	116.3	119.4	125.5	128.6	131.6	134.7
125	75	81.2	87.5	93.7	100	106.2	112.5	115.6	118.7	121.8	128.1	131.2	134.3	137.4
127.5	76.5	82.8	89.2	95.6	102	108.3	114.7	117.9	121.1	124.3	130.6	133.8	137	140.2
130	78	84.5	91	97.5	104	110.5	117	120.2	123.5	126.7	133.2	136.5	139.7	143
132.5	79.5	86.1	92.7	99.3	106	112.6	119.2	122.5	125.8	129.1	135.8	139.1	142.4	145.7
135	81	87.7	94.5	101.2	108	114.7	121.5	124.8	128.2	131.6	138.3	141.7	145.1	148.5
137.5	82.5	89.3	96.2	103.1	110	116.8	123.7	127.1	130.6	134	140.9	144.3	147.8	151.2
140	84	91	98	105	112	119	126	129.4	133	136.5	143.5	147	150.5	154
142.5	85.5	92.6	99.7	106.8	114	121.1	128.2	131.8	135.2	138.9	146	149.6	153.1	156.7
145	87	94.2	101.5	108.7	116	123.2	130.5	134.1	137.7	141.3	148.6	152.2	155.8	159.5
147.5	88.5	95.8	103.2	110.6	118	125.3	132.7	136.4	140.1	143.8	151.1	154.8	158.5	162.2
150	90	97.5	105	112.5	120	127.5	135	138.7	142.5	146.2	153.7	157.5	161.2	165
152.5	91.5	99.1	106.7	114.3	122	129.6	137.2	141	144.8	148.6	156.2	160.1	163.8	167.7
155	93	100.7	108.5	116.2	124	131.7	139.8	143.3	147.2	151	158.8	162.7	166.5	170.5
157.5	94.5	102.3	110.2	118.1	126	133.8	141.7	145.6	149.6	153.5	161.3	165.3	169.2	173.2
160	96	104	112	120	128	136	144	147.9	152	155.9	163.9	168	171.9	176
162.5	97.5	105.6	113.7	121.8	130	138.1	146.2	150.2	154.3	158.3	166.5	170.6	174.6	178.7
165	99	107.2	115.5	123.7	132	140.2	148.5	152.5	155.7	160.8	169	173.2	177.3	181.5
167.5	100.5	108.8	117.2	126.6	134	142.3	150.7	154.8	159.1	163.2	171.6	175.8	180	184.2
170	102	110.5	119	127.5	136	144.5	153	157.2	161.5	165.6	174.2	178.5	182.7	187
172.5	103.5	112.1	120.7	129.3	138	146.6	155.2	159.5	163.9	168.1	176.7	181.1	185.5	189.7
175	105	113.7	122.5	131.2	140	148.7	157.5	161.8	166.2	170.6	179.3	183.7	188.1	192.5
177.5	106	115.3	124.2	133.1	142	150.3	159.7	164.1	169.5	173	181.8	186.3	190.7	195.1
180	108	117	126	135	144	153	162	166.5	171	175.5	184.5	189	193.5	198
182.5	109.5	118.6	127.7	136.4	146	155.1	164.2	168.7	173.3	177.9	187	191.5	196.1	200.7
185	111	120.2	129.5	138.7	148	157.2	166.5	171.1	175.7	180.3	189.6	194.2	198.8	203.4
187.5	112.5	121.8	131.2	140.6	150	159.3	168.7	173.4	178	182.7	192.1	196.8	201.4	206.1
190	114	123.5	133	142.5	152	161.5	171	175.7	180.4	185.1	194.5	199.2	203.9	208.6
192.5	115.5	125.1	134.7	144.3	154	163.6	173.2	178	182.8	187.6	197.2	202	206.8	211.7
195	117	126.7	136.5	146.2	156	165.7	175.5	180.3	185.2	190.1	199.8	204.7	209.5	214.4
197.5	118.5	128.3	138.2	148.1	159	167.8	177.6	182.5	187.4	192.4	202.2	207.2	212.1	217
200	120	130	140	150	160	170	180	185	190	195	205	210	215	220
202.5	121.5	131.6	141.7	151.8	162	172.1	182.2	187.3	192.3	197.4	207.5	212.5	217.6	222.7
205	123	133.2	143.5	153.7	164	174.2	184.5	189.6	194.7	199.8	210.1	215.2	220.3	225.4
207.5	124.5	134.5	145.2	155.6	165	176.3	186.7	191.9	197	202.2	212.6	217.8	222.9	228.1
210	126	136.5	147	157.5	168	178.5	189	194.2	199.5	204.7	215.2	220.5	225.7	231
212.5	127.5	138.1	148.7	159.3	170	180.5	191.2	196.5	201.8	207.1	217.7	223	228.3	233.7
215	129	139.7	150.5	161.2	173	182.7	193.5	198.8	204.2	209.6	220.3	225.7	230	236.4
217.5	130.5	141.3	152.2	163.1	174	184.8	195.7	201.1	206.5	212	222.8	228.3	233.7	239.1
220	132	143	154	165	176	187	198	203.5	209	214.5	225.5	231	236.5	242
222.5	133.5	144.6	155.7	166.8	173	189.1	200.2	205.7	211.3	216.9	228	233.5	239.1	244.2
225	135	146.2	157.5	168.7	180	191.2	202.5	209.1	213.7	219.3	230.6	236.2	241.3	247.4

TRAINING AND PREPARATION

Training for competition

Modern weight lifting demands the development of great athletic prowess. Not only must the weight lifter be very strong, but he must have highly developed technical ability, great speed and flexibility and specialised tolerance to and rapid recovery from very heavy and hard work (overload). The lifter must also be courageous and single-minded. Weight-lifting training places great pressure on the lifter through the massive quantities of very hard work that must be performed. Weight lifting is a true and challenging test of athletic ability and from the beginner's earliest days of training, programmes will be designed to develop these strength abilities progressively and purposefully.

Training the beginner

In the majority of cases, the beginner in the sport will be very young; within the rules of B.A.W.L.A., competition at school level may begin at thirteen years of age. This will require the lifter to have had a year's previous training in order to have learned the movements and to have made sufficient progress to achieve the qualifying totals necessary for selection to the British Championships.

In some eastern European countries, where weight lifting is regarded as a national sport, youngsters are subject to a very early selection process in which both their physical and psychological potential are measured. Those found suitable attend special weight-lifting schools at the age of twelve and follow a programme until such time as they are drafted into the armed forces and colleges of physical education. This means, of course, that they are full time weight lifters for all of their young lives.

Whether a form of selection for youngsters is possible in western countries is doubtful and there are uncertainties as to the advisability of such ideas and their application. The coach is therefore likely to have a mixture of youngsters coming to the club for training, some with far greater potential than others. But in order to make certain that each candidate can fully enjoy the sport, his approach must be the same for all. Not everyone who takes up the sport will be a champion; but all can derive a great deal of pleasure and sense of achievement, especially if they are taught correctly from the outset.

The main areas that must be covered in the beginner's programme are as follows.

1   The development of correct technique.
2   The development of power.
3   The development of positive attitudes towards competition.

The development of correct technique

As far as the development of correct technique is concerned, it is essential that the coach has in his mind's eye a very clear picture of the requirements of each lift and that he translates this when teaching.

I have suggested, for instance, that a novice's first taught movement should be the jerk above the head in the split position; this will ensure that the essential mobility of the hip region is established before the flexibility restrictions inherent in squat technique dominate the movement. The correct manoeuvre can then be built up via the specialised assistance exercise of the jerk balance (see page 57).

Naturally, the positional aspects of the snatch – which also require great flexibility, particularly in the upper spine – will play an important role in early learning; the snatch balance exercises (see pages 29–32) are ideal in teaching this complicated technique. Technical exercises must take on primary importance in the first schedules that confront the lifter.

The development of power

It is understandable that a youngster wishes to test his strength and this instinct should not be suppressed. Since strength is at the sport's core, power development must be built into early training schedules, engaged mainly through exercises that are 'massive' in nature, i.e. those which affect large muscle groups. Our study of technique shows that force must be accumulated through carefully linked muscular activity, with the result that major muscle groups act before the smaller and less powerful ones. Initial emphasis is therefore thrown on the legs, hips and back. Since these muscle groups

– working in sequence – perform the action of the lift, this is a very important movement on which to concentrate.

The basic flat back starting position should be introduced, leading to the pull to maximum upward extension. Providing the lifter maintains the flat back position and is coached in the correct sequence of muscular movement, this exercise can become a vital early power builder. Front and back squats should also be brought into the schedule from the start because the benefits of increasing leg strength will pay rapid dividends.

Coaches must remember that the first movements learned will remain with the lifter forever. If, despite future careful coaching, they are incorrect, the lifter is liable to revert to them under conditions of stress such as major competition. It is essential, therefore, that all coaching for technique and power development is presented gradually and carefully, with the lifter being allowed to progress only when the coach is satisfied that each stage has been mastered.

The development of positive attitudes towards competition

From as early a stage as possible, the young lifter must be given clear, realistic aims. These fall into two groups: firstly, the development of correct technique and increasing power; secondly, preparation for the first competition. The positive approach to competition will be very much enhanced by successful technical and power training. The coach must give positive reinforcement at all levels of coaching, ensuring that these physical aspects are built up steadily and correctly. In this way, the athlete will look forward to lifting in competition and will expect success either as a winner or in achieving new best results.

Since the environment of the competition differs from the normal training situation, some time must be devoted to describing and rehearsing the nature of the requirements of the contest. The lifter should certainly have attempted near maximum lifts successfully in training about ten days prior to the competition. These achievements should be seen as possible second attempts during the contest. First attempts must always be with a weight that, whilst challenging, will not present the lifter with too much difficulty. In this way, he may move through the contest and achieve positive results on which subsequent training plans can be based.

The first schedule

The first schedule is based upon the technical learning process and as such will concentrate on the jerk and the snatch. I am of the belief that four training sessions per week is a realistic schedule with which to begin; this enables the coach to employ an alternating schedule system from the start. This system comprises two schedules which are used on alternate days as follows: schedule A on Monday, schedule B on Tuesday, schedule A on Thursday, schedule B on Friday. The intermediate days are devoted to recovery and free exercise.

Schedule A

1	Warm-up	Mobility exercise especially important
2	Jerk balance exercises	5 sets of 3 repetitions
3	Snatch pulls	5 × 5
4	Front squats	5 × 5
5	Abdominal work	

Schedule B

1	Warm-up	Mobility exercise especially important
2	Snatch balance exercises	5 sets of 3 repetitions
3	Clean pulls	5 × 5
4	Back squats	5 × 5
5	Hyperextensions	

This system is very simple to follow and the emphasis should be on learning the basic technical positions. It will last for about four weeks, depending on the lifter's progress, which often will be related to his improving flexibility. At the end of this period the system will be extended by the introduction of the power snatch to schedule A and the power clean to schedule B. These will be the second exercises in each schedule with the technical learning exercise of the jerk balance and the snatch balance exercises being prominent. These last two exercises will therefore remain first in the schedule so that they are performed when the lifter is least fatigued.

The mid-point free day (Wednesday) is programmed for recovery and within this a certain amount of physiological compensation will occur, recharging the lifter for the Thursday and Friday sessions. In the past it was thought that a rest day had to be taken between each schedule. It is now known that more frequent repetitions of the schedule create an adaption to overload within the body, making progress more rapid. We shall see that these principles of adaption are developed considerably in more advanced schedules. A rest day between schedules, in fact, acts as a break in progress and so it is now acceptable to train even beginners in blocks of two consecutive days.

The weekend free days (Saturday and Sunday) will provide an excellent opportunity for more general training, especially that which will place overload on the cardio-vascular and circulo-respiratory system. The choice is very wide and may include games with low injury potential, swimming, running (especially short sprints), field athletics and gymnastics. The latter two are especially valuable since many of the qualities inherent in these sports are very similar to those in weight lifting. Exercises of special value to fitness for weight lifting will be of a short duration and explosive in nature. Short sprinting, standing high and long jumps, shot throwing with both hands backwards over the head and specialised stretching exercises of a non-ballistic nature will play an important role in general training.

It may well be the case that young lifters have had their first introduction to lifting through the B.A.W.L.A. clean and jerk competition for schoolchildren. If they have not competed in this event, it is definitely worth considering at this early stage as a very valuable assistance to enthusiasm and, indeed, as a taste of that which is to come. The scheme has its own officer who should be contacted for the appropriate entry forms. B.A.W.L.A. has other schools schemes and by progressing through the various levels, the young lifter will be provided with a controlled and progressive scheme of achievement.

It is most important as progress is made that the young lifter is able to measure his success; this will be strongly motivational. The coach must demonstrate his pleasure in the lifting technique. A lifter's technique must be praised and rewarded more than the amount of weight he is able to lift. It is essential that realistic aims are set and achieved as a progressive stage in future designs.

Always guard against the negative effects that can emanate from lack of control of enthusiasm from the young lifter or from others associated with him, especially parents. The young lifter is not fully mature, either physically or mentally, and his view of his capabilities may well be exaggerated. He is also likely to give up if things don't seem to be going his way. Many of these problems are associated with the changes that occur as he moves from a child to a young adult and are physiological and psychological in nature. A correctly balanced and graduated programme of effort with success built into its framework will help him to get through to the next stage of training when the physical demands of the sport will increase considerably.

Youth training: age 16–18

During this period the lifter moves through adolescence into early adulthood and the approach to the overload ought to be altered, placing far greater emphasis on the development of power. Providing the technique of the lift has been mastered and the coach is satisfied that the standard of performance of the assistance exercises is related sufficiently to technical pathways, programmes can be based on the following criteria.

1   The lifter should be able to increase the amount of training time devoted to the development of power.

2   As the tempo and loading of the schedules increases, the amount of time devoted to fitness training can be reduced. 'Weight-lifting fitness' will be developed by the nature of the training programmes.

3   The coach must ensure that technical pathways are not lost or compromised by the greater increase in the concentration on power development.

4   The coach must prepare the schedules and programmes and these must be under his control. Often the young lifter, if left to devise his own training, will overestimate his capabilities and prepare work-outs that he will not be able to sustain.

5   Competitions, 'try-outs' and attempts at new bests should be carefully built into the programme.

6   These must provide challenges, not only of a physical nature, but which help to develop hardness of character under stressful conditions. Success plays a very important part in this and is the best psychological reinforcement.

The coach also has the responsibility to 'look after' the young lifter. The sport should be fun and the lifter should want to lift, to train and enjoy the competitive situation. There are times, however, when problems may occur and the coach then has to take on a different role; it is the determination of the coach that will see the lifter through difficult times. The young lifter has to realise that if he wants to be a champion, it will require sacrifices and very hard work. It is often awkward for the coach, especially if the lifter has friends who seem to be enjoying a socially wider leisure time than his training will allow.

This period of the lifter's development is, in reality, the last time that the sound essential basis of technique can be laid down. It is most likely that errors in technique, if not corrected at this stage, will remain uncorrected. The programme therefore concentrates on: firstly, the development of skill, best augmented by the repetitive practice of specially designed assistance exercises which are part of the whole movement of the snatch and the clean and jerk and by the whole movements themselves; secondly, the development of power, best advanced by heavy resistance movements closely related to the classical lifts, both in part and in whole. These are massive dynamic movements and will take on greater and greater importance in the schedule as the lifter progresses.

The schedule will be based still upon the 'A-B' principle but an extra day of training should be included. We will refer to this as schedule C. Thus, the week's arrangement could be constructed as follows.

Monday	Schedule A
Tuesday	Schedule B
Wednesday	Rest
Thursday	Schedule A
Friday	Schedule B
Saturday	Schedule C
Sunday	Rest

The schedule for Saturday – Schedule C – will consist of power exercises only. This can be varied from one Saturday to the next but the nature of the exercises will remain the same, as follows.

Schedule C(1)	Schedule C(2)
Power snatch	Power clean
Clean grip pulls	Snatch grip pulls
Front squats	Back squats

At this stage, the repetitions will all be 5 sets of 3. The guides for the weight to be handled are as follows.

Clean grip pulls and snatch grip pulls
Set 1 – 20 kg below best clean or snatch
Set 2 – 10 kg below best clean or snatch
Set 3 – Best clean or snatch
Set 4 – 10 kg above best clean or snatch
Set 5 – 20 kg above best clean or snatch

Front squats
Set 1 – 20 kg below best clean
Set 2 – 10 kg below best clean
Set 3 – Best clean
Set 4 – 10 kg above best clean
Set 5 – 20 kg above best clean

Back squats
Set 1 – Best clean
Set 2 – 10 kg above best clean
Set 3 – 20 kg above best clean
Set 4 – 30 kg above best clean
Set 5 – 35 kg above best clean

It may be possible to increase to the 40 kg mark for the last set. However, if either the 35 kg increase or the 40 kg increase prove to be too difficult, then the 5th set can be a repetition of the 4th, i.e. 2 final sets at 30 kg above the lifter's best clean.

Schedule C should be performed on the Saturday; since this will mean that schedules A, B and C have been performed in block, it is essential that Sunday is a rest day in order to recover for the training cycle of the following week. (Schedules A and B retain the same construction as the beginner's first programme.)

Training lifters of intermediate standard

Lifters who are classified as of intermediate standard are those who have achieved divisional selection and representation. They should therefore be technically competent and be able to devote a greater part of the schedule and training plan to the development of power.

At this stage, it is important to study the development of training plans in the light of the sporting calendar and those competitions which lie within it and which are considered to be important in the general progressive development of the lifter. The preparation of schedules and training plans must be approached with a clear understanding of the aims and achievements expected of the lifter. Both the coach and the lifter should select the most important future competition for which the training is to be designed. This will depend on the achievement level of the lifter; for the intermediate standard lifter, this could well be the divisional or area championships.

Lifters who are more experienced may well look towards competitions of the highest level. For these athletes, the World Championships, Olympic Games and European Championships will constitute the main competitions within the calendar. The Commonwealth Games will also feature as a most important competition and may, for the less developed countries, provide lifting of a truly international flavour for lifters of intermediate qualification only. However, what is of great importance is that these competitions are viewed as a goal, an opportunity to achieve the best possible results. The lifter must be ambitious but the coach must control and guide him to a successful completion of the projected aims.

One such calendar for a lifter of an intermediate standard might be as follows.

Aim	Nature of aim	Date of championships
1st	Training build-up	(April 25th)
2nd	Club champion	July 5th
3rd	County champion	September 13th
Final	Divisional champion	November 30th

This programme sees the lifter aiming to become champion at the divisional championships in six months' time. Within this period he will have three intermediate aims: first, to build up his training tempo to achieve his second aim of becoming club champion; then, two repetitions of the process in order to become both county and divisional champion.

The coach and lifter therefore work backwards from the main selected competition. With the more advanced lifter, greater importance will be attached to the intermediate competitions as they may well be vital in the selection process for national representation. In addition, each of the intermediate competitions should produce a new best result. This is important because the new results will indicate the increases in loading that the lifter should be given for each of the build-up stages. It is essential therefore that success is built into programmes and schedules. This involves realistic planning, both in the long term and in the shorter periods that make up the inter-mediate blocks of training prior to each competition.

The experience of coaches has shown that these intermediate blocks of training should last for about 10 to 12 weeks and that competitions and try-outs should come at the end of each of these periods. In our plan for the intermediate standard lifter aiming to become divisional champion, we would therefore have the following blocks of training: April 25th to July 5th – 10 weeks, July 5th to September 13th – 10 weeks, September 13th to November 30th – 11 weeks.

These blocks will be divided in 2 phases. phase 1 is called the 'preparation phase' and phase 2 is called the 'competition phase'. Each of the phases will last for 5 weeks. With the more advanced lifter, the preparation phase will last for 7 weeks. Further illustration of our intermediate plan would therefore look like this.

Block	Phase	Length	Phase	Length	Aim
1	Preparation	5 weeks	Competition	5 weeks	Club chmps
2	Preparation	5 weeks	Competition	5 weeks	County chmps
	One week of active rest				
3	Preparation	5 weeks	Competition	5 weeks	Divisional chmps

It is important to remember that often the dates of major competitions do not correspond exactly with the ideal arrangements with which we would like to plan. In the above example, since there is an 11 week period between the county championships and the divisional championships, a week's active rest has been planned immediately following the former. This will allow for recuperation before the final and most important block of training, prior to the divisional championships. The coach must always consider these timings and where no official competition is scheduled to coincide with the end of each block, some try-outs must be programmed to give purpose and set figures for the subsequent load planning.

Let us look in a little more detail at the two phases of training build-up.

The preparation phase

The bulk of training is carried out during this period. It is initially a period of quantity in loading and the athlete is expected to undertake large blocks of work with comparatively high repetitions. Most exercises will therefore be performed in 5 sets of 5 repetitions. This gives the coach the opportunity to check on the technical progress of the lifter and to correct any errors that may exist.

Since the weight will be comparatively light and the repetitions high, this is the ideal time for such technical coaching. In addition, this type of loading will develop high levels of power and lifting-related endurance. This relates to the specialised weight-lifting fitness that is essential in the development of rapid recovery from the very heavy loading of one work-out to the next that makes up the bulk of the competition phase.

The competition phase

This phase can be considered as a rehearsal for the conditions to come. These conditions apply to the actual competition and therefore the tempo and increase in the resistance handled will benefit the lifter both physically and psychologically. A far greater emphasis is placed upon the classical lifts and those assistance exercises which are very much a part of the snatch and the clean and jerk. The quantity of the work is generally reduced whilst the quality or intensity is increased. This means that whilst resistance in the range of 70% to 90% of best results and related exercises is used in the preparatory phase, a much greater emphasis is placed on maximum resistance in the range of 90% to 100% for the competitive phase.

At certain stages of the phase, weights – especially for the snatch, the clean and jerk and squatting – will be advanced to over 100%. In fact, to new best results. This is especially valuable to the lifter because he must come to terms with the stressful aspects of lifting very heavy weights. Whilst this experience is not identical to competition, it will nevertheless be a strong psychological reinforcement for the lifter. This is very important and has been built into the training of lifters for the purpose of developing 'the will'. In the past, it was thought that to lift at maximum more than a few times a year would damage a lifter's progress. Now many lifters attempt maximums several times every week with a special period in each week's training planned as 'stress days', when intensity is very high.

The last 3 weeks of this period are very important. Week 8 should see the intermediate standard lifter aiming for over 100% of best results in the snatch, the clean and jerk and the squat. Weeks 9 and 10 are very much the final rehearsal for the competition at the end of the tenth week, i.e. the divisional championships. Success is essential at this time – failure should be minimised. All techniques should be very sound and the lifter should be building up his reserves of energy and be very confident in his approach to the forthcoming competition.

Week 8 is the final week in which the very heaviest weights are lifted. Here new bests can and *should* be attempted. The ninth week should see the lifter working at the level of the weights that he hopes to lift as first attempts in the competition. Squatting and pulling movements should be in the range of 95% of previous best results for squatting and up to 20 kg above best clean and snatch results. This will allow the work to be very positive and dynamic with strong competitive elements built in.

The final week prior to the competition day is a 'tapering off' period. All training must be very accurate and the emphasis is on building up reserves of energy for the competition. The bodyweight must be checked frequently and appropriate adjustments made. In general, the advice given to lifters of this standard is to have two clear days of rest prior to the competition. However, some lifters feel that this is too long and a very light work-out may be taken, allowing one clear day of rest before the match. This is perfectly acceptable since the tempo of modern lifting means that lifters are more used to regular repeated training day after day.

The outline of the intermediate training plan for each block of competition build-up will follow this arrangement.

Preparation period: 5 weeks

	Week 1	Week 2	Week 3	Week 4	Week 5
Sets & reps	5×5	5×5	5×5	a) 3×3 b) 3×3	a) 3×5 b) 5×3
% of best lifts	70%	80%	75%	a) 80% b) 85%	a) 80% b) 90%
Back squats	5×3 70%	5×3 80%	5×3 75%	5×3 85%	5×3 90%

Competition period: 5 weeks

	Week 6	Week 7	Week 8
Sets & reps	5×3 3×2 5 singles	5×3 3×2	5×3 3×2 5 singles
% heaviest set	85%	82.5%	90%
Single lifts	97.5%		100+%
Back squats	5×2 90%	5×3 85%	2×2 90% 2×2 95% 3 singles to 100% +

Tapering down

Week 9 Olympic lifts: to starting weight (1st attempt). Other lifts: in range to 95%.
  Note Correct technique. Adequate rest. Bodyweight control.

Week 10 Olympic lifts: snatch 10 kg below starting kg. Clean & jerk 80%–90%. Other lifts: light & fast. Related to Olympic lifts. Squats: reps of 2 and singles 85%.
  Note Correct technique. Adequate rest. Bodyweight control.

Remember that gains in strength can hardly be expected during the last week of training in a 10 week programme. All lifts are a rehearsal for competition. They need, however, to be realistic in terms of resistance.

On the day of competition, the lifter must check all his personal kit and equipment, arrive at the correct time for the weigh-in and ensure that he has all the necessary drinks and easily digested high energy foods that he may desire. This is his big day – he must concentrate but be calm. He must also listen to the coach – who will have control of his involvement within the competition – and focus on success.

Based upon the recommendations for the selection of repetitions and resistance, the following programme may be pursued.

Weeks 1–5 Preparation phase 4 times per week training

Day 1	Day 2	Day 3	Day 4
Snatch	Snatch balance	Snatch balance	Power snatch
Power cleans	Snatch pulls	Power cleans	Snatch pulls
Clean pulls	Front squats	Clean pulls	Heave press
Jerk from rack	Heave press	Jerk from rack	Front squats
Back squats	Hyperextensions	Back squats	Hyperextensions
Abdominals		Abdominals	

Weeks 6–8 Competition phase 4 times per week training

Day 1	Day 2	Day 3	Day 4
Snatch	Clean & jerk	Snatch	Clean & jerk
Power cleans	Snatch balance	Power cleans	Power snatch
Clean pulls	Snatch pulls	Heave jerk	Snatch pulls
Jerk from rack	Back squats	Front squats	Press
Front squats	Hyperextensions	Abdominals	Hyperextensions
Abdominals			

Weeks 9–10 Competition phase
Week 9

Day 1	Day 2	Day 3	Day 4
Snatch	Clean & jerk	Power snatch	Snatch
Snatch pulls	Clean pulls	Power cleans	Clean & jerk
Front squats	Back squats	Front squats	Back squats
Abdominals	Hyperextensions		

Week 10 Taper off

Day 1 (Mon)	Day 2 (Tues)	Day 3 (Wed)	Day 4 (Thurs)
Snatch	Clean & jerk	Power snatch	Play with
Snatch pulls	Clean pulls	Power clean & jerk	empty bar
Front squats	Back squats	Light single back squats	

Day 5 (Fri)	Day 6
Rest	Competition

Training lifters of advanced qualification

The necessity for long-term planning is essential when dealing with lifters of national standard. A major competition will be in the mind of both the lifter and the coach and all preparation will relate to this. It is therefore essential that all build-ups are directed to the very best possible result in this major competition. Intermediate competitions will hold great importance also and will be seen as stages of development in terms of results and the selection process.

Whilst the arrangements and timing of international competition do not always fit in exactly with the ideal block of 10 weeks, the coach must bear in mind adjustments that will always retain a fixed period for the competitive phase, with reductions or additions in training being made to the preparation phase. In this way, an 8 week block of training could be 4 weeks preparation phase, 4 weeks competitive phase. A 10 week block would consist of 6 weeks preparation phase, 4 weeks competitive phase. If it is necessary, due to longer periods between competitions, a 12 week block would be constructed of 8 weeks preparation phase and 4 weeks competitive phase. Longer periods than this should be broken up by arranging try-outs in place of competitions. This would be built into the plan and so spaced that the period after the try-out would be for a block of 10 weeks. In this way, if the lifter was 16 weeks away from the main competition, a plan such as this could be prepared – 6 weeks preparation, with the tryout at the end of the sixth week, followed by a 10 week block of training to the major competition.

The try-out is likely to produce new best results which could then be used to influence the percentages of workload for individual movements in the 10 week block of training which will follow. The try-out must be regarded as only a work-out under these circumstances. No special build-up or 'psyche-up' should be undertaken and the 10 week block of training will follow immediately. Following major competitions, however, a week of active rest (light exercise of a recuperative nature – no heavy lifting) must be undertaken. This is to allow for essential recovery from both physical and mental stress that the demands of major competitions place upon the lifter.

The long-term plans which are used for the blocks of training will follow certain patterns as well. The first of these is outlined below and was followed with great success by many lifters during the late 1960's and early 1970's. Since the tempo and tolerance for greater loading have increased considerably since that time, this programme would be recommended for lifters just entering the elite classification and may well form the basis of their first year of hard and very serious training. The plan is based on an 'A-B' schedule construction and would be followed on that basis, irrespective of the days of the week.

Mon	– Schedule A	Sun	– Schedule A
Tues	– Schedule B	Mon	– Schedule B
Wed	– Rest	Tues	– Rest
Thurs	– Schedule A	Wed	– Schedule A
Fri	– Schedule B	Thurs	– Schedule B
Sat	– Rest	Fri	– Rest, and so on

This plan necessitates that training facilities be available 7 days of the week and is suited to a lifter capable of a 90 kg snatch and a 120 kg clean and jerk. In order to bring the plan in line with the 10 week training block, it is arranged as follows.

Schedule A	70%–80%	80%–90%	90%–100%
12 week plan	4 weeks	4 weeks	4 weeks
10 week plan	3 weeks	3 weeks	4 weeks
	Kg reps	Kg reps	Kg reps
Snatch	55×5	65×3	70×3
	65×5	75×3	82.5×3
	75×5	87.5×3	90×3
	60×5	70×3	75×3
Clean grip pulls	85×5	90×5	106×3
	90×5	100×5	115×3
	100×5	110×5	120×3
			125×3
	90×5	100×5	130×3
Jerk (power)	85×3	90×2	100×2
	90×3	100×2	110×2
	100×3	110×2	120×2
	90×3	95×2	110×2
Front squats	100×5	105×5	105×3
			115×3
	110×5	115×5	120×3
			125×3
	120×5	125×5	130×3
Trunk forward bend	(Light×10)3	(Medium×5)3	(Heavy×5)3

Schedule B	70%–80%	80%–90%	90%–100%
12 week plan	4 weeks	4 weeks	4 weeks
10 week plan	3 weeks	3 weeks	4 weeks
	Kg reps	Kg reps	Kg reps
Clean & jerk	85×3	90×2	100×2
(Jerk last	90×3	100×2	110×2
rep only)	100×3	110×2	120×2
	90×3	95×2	110×2
Snatch grip pulls	50×5	60×5	70×3
	60×5	70×5	80×3
	70×5	80×5	90×3
			95×3
	60×5	70×5	100×3
Snatch balance	70×3	75×3	80×3
	80×3	85×3	90×3
	90×3	95×3	100×3
	75×3	80×3	90×3

Power snatch	50×3	55×3	60×3
	55×3	60×3	70×3
	60×3	65×3	75×3
	50×3	60×3	65×3
Back squats	120×3	125×3	130×3
	125×3	130×3	135×3
	130×3	135×3	140×3
			145×3
			150×3
Abdominals	(Free×5)5	(5 kg×5)5	(10 kg×5)10

During the penultimate week of the competitive phase, single maximum attempts of 100% and over could be attempted. The final week is a tapering down period (see page 84).

The standard of lifting here indicates that the lifter would be either in the 56 kg class (bantam weight) or at the early days of competition in the 60 kg class (feather weight). He would therefore be a very good and developing junior who would likely be national champion and aiming for a 255 kg total in 18 months' time. (Such arrangements as these can of course be planned for any competitions at any time.)

A 12 week version of this type of plan is also illustrated and again indicates the progressive development through the preparation phase (weeks 1 to 8) and the competitive period (weeks 9 to 12). For some time the 10 week block of training has proved to be very popular. Two examples are given.

Example 1

Date		Week 1	Week 2	Week 3	Week 4	Week 5	Week 6	Week 7	Week 8	Week 9	Week 10
		All exercises 5 sets of 5 reps after warm-up at % of best for each exercise				3×5 and 5×3	5×3 and 5 single attempts	3×5 and 5×3	5×3 and 5 single attempts	Olympic lifts to starter or 10 kg below	Very light
DAY 1	Snatch balance	70%	75%	72.5%	80%	Top set 80%	Top set 85% Singles to 95%	Top set 82.5%	Top set 90% Singles to 100% or new best	Snatch 3×3,5×1 Snatch pull 3×3,5×2 Front/split squats 3×3,5×1 Hyperextensions	To starter 5×2 5×1
	Power snatch	70%	75%	72.5%	80%	80%		''			
	Snatch pull	70%	75%	72.5%	80%	80%	''	''			
	Front or split squats	70%	75%	72.5%	80%	80%	''	''	''		
	Press behind neck	70%	75%	72.5%	80%	80%	''	''	''		
DAY 2	Power clean	70%	75%	72.5%	80%	80%	''	''	''	Clean and jerk 3×3,5×1	To starter 5×2 5×1
	Clean pull	70%	75%	72.5%	80%	80%	''	''	''	Clean pull 3×3,5×2	
	Jerk									Back squats	

	from rack	70%	75%	72.5%	80%	80%	"	"	"	3×3,5×1 Hyperextensions
	Back squat	70%	75%	72.5%	80%	80%	"	"	"	
	Hyperex-tensions	70%	75%	72.5%	80%	80%	"	"	"	
DAY 3	Snatch	70%	75%	72.5%	80%	80%	"	"	"	Power snatch 3×3,3×2 Power clean and jerk 3×3,3×2
	Clean	70%	75%	72.5%	80%	80%	"	"	"	
	Snatch pull	70%	75%	72.5%	80%	80%	"	"	"	Rest
	Clean pull	70%	75%	72.5%	80%	80%	"	"	"	
	Abdom-inals	70%	75%	72.5%	80%	80%	"	"	"	
DAY 4	As day 1	70%	75%	72.5%	80%	80%	"	"	"	Power snatch 3×3,5×1 Power clean 3×3,5×1 Front/split squats 3×3,5×1	Rest
DAY 5	As day 2	70%	75%	72.5%	80%	80%	"	"	"	Snatch 3×3,5×1 Clean and jerk 3×3,5×1	Rest
COMPETITION DAY										Championship

The loading of the second example is greater and therefore of a more advanced construction.

Example 2
Preparation phase 5 weeks

	Week 1	Week 2	Week 3	Week 4	Week 5
Sets & reps	5×5	5×5	5×5	4×3 & 4×3	3×5 & 5×3
% of best lifts	70	80	75	80 & 85	80 & 90
All squats (back & front) 5×3	70%	80%	75%	85%	90%

Competition phase

	Week 6	Week 7	Week 8	
Sets & reps	5×3 3×2 5 singles	5×3 3×2	5×3 3×2 5 singles	
% heaviest set	85	82.5	90	
Single lifts	97.5		100+	
All squats (back & front)	5×2 95%	5×3 85%	2×2 2×2 3 singles – 100%+	90% 95%

Tapering down week 9
Olympic lifts to selected starting weight for snatch and clean and jerk. All other lifts to the range 95%. The emphasis in this week's training is on correct technique and build-up of reserves. Check bodyweight.

Week 10

| Olympic lifts | Snatch 10 kg below selected starting weight. Clean and jerk to around 85%. Other lifts light and fast. |
| Back squats | To around 80%. One day rest before competition. Check bodyweight. |

In all of these plans the choice of exercises will depend upon any particular weaknesses that the lifter may display. However, the layouts given may be followed by the great majority of lifters. Included here at this stage of the planning is a more detailed view of the variations of the last four weeks of the training programme. This is a very important period and the variations shown are for both advanced lifters and lifters who are approaching that standard.

Breakdown of the last month's competitive phase prior to competition

Lifters of 1st class qualification

Week 1 (7)	Week 2 (8)	Week 3 (9)	Week 4 (10)
Light volume	Medium volume	Heavy intensity Low repetitions Heavy weights	Day 1 Medium heavy intensity Day 2 Rest Day 3 Very light 10 kg below starting weight Day 4 Rest Day 5 Rest Day 6 Competition

Lifters of advanced qualification

Week 1 (7)	Week 2 (8)	Week 3 (9)	Week 4 (10)
Medium volume	Heavy intensity Top set 90% Singles 100+%	Olympic lifts to starting weight All other lifts to 95%	Final week – advanced Day 1 Snatch 10 kg below starting weight Day 2 Clean & jerk 85% Back squats 80% Day 3 Rest Day 4 Very light training Day 5 Rest (free exercise or bar only) Day 6 Competition

Very advanced training is based upon the weight-lifting school systems in Bulgaria. This would require full-time training. The workload is very great and the intensity at maximum. The first outline is for this type of training on a 'twice-per-day basis' and the second illustration is for a lifter who can train once per day but who would have good opportunities for rest and recovery.

The programme is dependent on rest periods of 30 minutes between lifts and is planned thus.

Daily programme
Monday, Wednesday and Friday

Morning
On Mondays, Wednesdays and Fridays the training session begins at 9.00 a.m. on the following schedule.

1 Front squat – Max. for that day – 2 attempts. Down 10 kg. 3 × 1.

2 Snatch – Max.
If the maximum attempt is above the previous maximum weight, the attempt is not repeated. If the weight is within the abilities of the competitor, and a failed lift is due to a technical mistake or insufficient mobilisation and determination, the attempt may be repeated until eventual success, but not more than 3–4 times. Come down 5 kg for 2 attempts × 1. Very often after maximum attempts, a psychological relief sets in, and the attempts at 5 kg below are not successful. The weight lifter must work until 2 successful attempts are achieved. Come down 10 kg for 3 successful singles. The repeats hold for all the exercises.

3 Clean and jerk – (snatch same procedure). There is a 30 minute break-time between the squat, snatch and clean and jerk exercises. This pause is necessary not only to provide physical rest, but also in order to assure time for psychological readiness and adjustment for the following training and the following heavy weights which are in the competitor's schedule.

Afternoon (4.30 p.m.–5.00 p.m.)
1 Snatch
2 Clean and jerk
3 Squat
The exercises and the repetitions are the same. The only difference is that in the afternoon the training finishes with the squat.

Daily programme
Tuesday, Thursday and Saturday.

Morning
1 Power snatch
2 Power clean and jerk } 90 minutes

Afternoon
1 Squat
2 Snatch pull
3 Clean pull
} 90 minutes: 2 hours with 30 minute break after the squat. 5 sets of 5 at 10 kg above the best snatch and the best clean and jerk of the day before.

This describes the training during the heavy weeks. In addition there are light weeks. One light week follows two heavy weeks. The change in the programme for the light week is negligible. Instead of having repetitions of attempts at 5 kg and 10 kg after the maximal attempts, they are exchanged with attempts at 10 kg and 20 kg below maximal.

Besides the heavy and light weeks there is the tapering down week. This is the week following the last light week and includes the days before the competition. Careful individual coaching for each competitor is required during this last week. The correct evaluation of the training and the correct tapering down week lead up to stable and calm competition.

The possibilities of the last week must be positive, based upon the effectiveness of the work done previously and aim for high results.

Tapering down week – day-by-day

Monday	Morning	1	Front squat 90% 15 mins rest
		2	Snatch 85%–90% 30 mins rest
		3	Clean and jerk 80%–85%
	Afternoon	1	Snatch – max. 30 mins rest
		2	Clean and jerk 90% 15 mins rest
		3	Back squat – max.
Tuesday	Afternoon	1	Power snatch 80%–90% 30 mins rest

		2	Power clean 80%–90%
		3	Back squat
Wednesday	Morning	1	Front squat 90% 30 mins rest
		2	Snatch 90% 15 mins rest
		3	Clean and jerk 70%–80%
	Afternoon	1	Snatch – first and second attempt at the competition
		2	Clean and jerk – up to the last attempt of the warming up
		3	Back squat – max.
Thursday			Rest day
Friday			The day before competition, there may be short light training, usually according to the self-confidence of the competitor. The reduction in bodyweight is also taken into account (if any), as well as other details of the competition.
		1	Snatch 50%–70%
		2	Clean and jerk – individual
		3	Squat

This programme is outlined in detail as follows.

Training of advanced lifters

Here is the programme for a lifter (82.5 kg bodyweight) capable of: snatch 140 kg, clean and jerk 170 kg, front squat 200 kg, back squat 230 kg.

Weekly training – heavy weeks

Heavy days: Monday-Wednesday-Friday

9.00 a.m.   **1   Front squat** – To maximum (for that day) 2 attempts. Down to 10 kg – 3 single attempts.

Example   Max. 200 kg

```
 50 kg × 5 ⎫
 70 kg × 5 ⎪
100 kg × 3 ⎬ Warm-up
120 kg × 3 ⎪
140 kg × 3 ⎭
160 kg × 2
180 kg × 2 (if possible)
190 kg × 1
195 kg × 1
200 kg × 1 × 1 – then down 10 kg
190 kg × 1 × 1
```

If in the example the lifter failed 200 kg twice then the 10 kg drop-down would be from the last lift (i.e. 195 kg) to 185 kg for 3 singles. Total time for this exercise 30–35 minutes. Now rest 30 minutes.

2   Snatch

Example   Max. 140 kg

```
 50 kg × 3 ⎫
 70 kg × 3 ⎬ Warm-up
 90 kg × 3 ⎪
110 kg × 2 ⎭
120 kg × 1
130 kg × 1
135 kg × 1
140 kg × 1 × 1
135 kg × 1 × 1
130 kg × 1 × 1 × 1
```

Now rest 30 minutes.

3   Clean and jerk

Example   Max. 170 kg

```
 50 kg × 3 ⎫
 70 kg × 3 ⎬ Warm-up
 90 kg × 3 ⎪
110 kg × 3 ⎭
130 kg × 2
150 kg × 1
160 kg × 1
170 kg × 1 × 1
165 kg × 1 × 1
160 kg × 1 × 1 × 1 finish
```

Heavy weeks

Heavy days: Monday-Wednesday-Friday

4.30 p.m.   **1   Snatch** – same as training in morning

2   Clean and jerk – same as training in morning

3   Back squat

Example   230 kg maximum

150 kg ×3
170 kg ×3
190 kg ×2
210 kg ×2
220 kg ×1
230 kg ×1 ×1
220 kg ×1 ×1 ×1

30 minutes rest between exercises as per morning.

Heavy weeks

Light days: Tuesday-Thursday-Saturday

9.00 a.m.   **1   Power snatch** – same as for snatch (To maximum for 2 singles, then down 5 kg for 2 singles, then down 5 kg for 3 singles)

2   Power clean and jerk – same as for clean and jerk (To maximum for 2 singles, then down 5 kg for 2 singles, then down 5 kg for 2 singles)

30 minutes between exercises.

4.30 p.m.   **1   Back squat** – as before to maximum

2   Snatch pulls – 5×5
(150 kg)

2   Clean pulls – 5×5
(180 kg)
(At fixed weight of 10 kg more than best snatch and clean & jerk of day before.) To last 90–120 mins with 30 minute break after squats.

Weekly training – light weeks

All training is exactly the same as for the heavy weeks, i.e. to maximums. After maximums the lifter drops down 10 kg × 2 singles – then down 10 kg × 3 singles.

1   The tapering down week is fully described in the general description of this programme.
2   Technique training must be with realistic weights.
3   In the event of a substantial new maximum (the lifter must constantly try for new maximums), the reduction may be greater than 5 kg. This will take into account the great psychological effort of achieving new best results.

One of the main problems that face lifters is that, for many, it is impossible to train twice a day. The following programme caters for this problem. The principles and loadings are exactly the same as in previous descriptions, but we are now forced to increase to 4 exercises on Monday and Thursday, including pulls within the one schedule per day. It is also very important to note that on Saturday and Sunday the lifter must undertake to train twice as per the original schedule.

Example of programme for lifter who can train once per day except Saturday and Sunday

Monday	1	Back squat
	2	Snatch
	3	Clean and jerk
	4	Snatch pulls
Tuesday		Rest
Wednesday	1	Front squat
	2	Snatch
	3	Clean and jerk
Thursday	1	Back squat
	2	Power snatch
	3	Power clean and jerk
	4	Clean pulls
Friday	1	Front squat
	2	Snatch
	3	Clean and jerk
Saturday		Morning
	1	Front squat
	2	Power snatch
	3	Power clean and jerk
		Afternoon
	1	Back squat
	2	Snatch pulls
	3	Clean and jerk pulls

Sunday   Morning
1 Front squats
2 Snatch
3 Clean and jerk
Afternoon
1 Snatch
2 Clean and jerk
3 Back squat

Russian squatting programme

It is always very important to remember that the core of power in all lifting is centred around the leg-hip and lower-back area of the body.

Bearing this in mind, special squatting programmes can be followed in conjunction with other lifting exercises. The most popular programme is called the 'Russian squatting plan', named after its country of origin.

This programme can be used for front or back squats. It is followed three times per week for 6 weeks and must be finished at least 4 weeks prior to a major competition. This means that it is part of the preparation phase only. It fits ideally into a 12 week block of training. The first two sets are always as follows.

Set 1: 2 reps at 70%. Set 2: 2 reps at 75%. These can be considered as warm-up sets. The plan is as follows.

Week	Session			Sets/Reps	Resistance
1	1	2 reps 70%	2 reps 75%	6×2	80%
	2	''	''	6×3	80%
	3	''	''	6×2	80%
2	4	''	''	6×4	80%
	5	''	''	6×2	80%
	6	''	''	6×5	80%
3	7	''	''	6×2	80%
	8	''	''	6×6	80%
	9	''	''	6×2	80%
4	10	''	''	5×5	85%
	11	''	''	6×2	80%
	12	''	''	4×4	90%
5	13	''	''	6×2	80%
	14	''	''	3×3	95%
	15	''	''	6×2	80%
6	16	''	''	2×2	100%
	17	''	''	6×2	80%
	18	''	''	1 single rep	105%

Training methods – conclusion

It is always very important to remember that real progress can only be made when the relationship between technique and planning is realistic and correctly balanced. This means that the coach should coach all movements (including the assistance exercises) and that the coach and lifter should plan towards the major

competitions in the lifter's calendar of events.

The section on advanced training presents programmes that can only be followed by the very experienced and those with high levels of weight-lifting adaption to very heavy loading. All training is progressive. The lifter must set himself the highest goals. The best motivation is the success of the training plans.

DRUG ABUSE

One of the most serious problems to have damaged modern sport is the taking of drugs in an attempt to improve performance. Unfortunately, weight lifting has suffered more than most other sports. Weight lifters have brought great disgrace upon themselves, their countries and their sport. The sport is now under great pressure with demands that it should be taken out of the Olympics and other major international games. Should this happen, the sport would be in great danger of dying.

Drug abuse is very dangerous to your health – serious physical damage is a very real risk. That some sportsmen and women have died as a result of drug abuse is well documented. How very tragic that this should happen to any young person involved in activity that is supposed to promote health.

The abuse of drugs is **cheating**, against all the principles, rules and regulations of sport and sportsmanship. All participants must enter competition on an equal footing. Sport is about friendship and trust. A cheat is not a sportsman.

Doping control in sport

The information below is taken verbatim from a leaflet issued by the Sports Council called 'Doping control in sport'.

Why the concern about drugs in sport?
Drugs and other substances are now being taken not for the purposes they were intended, but simply to attempt to enhance performance in sport. It puts the health of the athlete at risk. It can be **dangerous**. It undermines the foundation of fair competition. It is **cheating**.

The only legitimate use of drugs in sport is for a medically justified purpose under the supervision of a doctor. Even here medicines should be sought which do not contravene the drug rules and stand no risk of causing harmful effects.

Governing bodies of sport, encouraged and assisted by the Sports Council, set up doping control to protect sportsmen and women from dangerous side effects and to prevent any unfair advantage which might be gained by cheats.

What is doping control?
It is a system whereby urine samples are collected, tested for banned substances and a disciplinary procedure followed if any are found. The aim is to eradicate the use of drugs to enhance performance.

Who will be tested?
One cannot know in advance who will be selected for drug testing. Selection is normally made at random on the day of competition or training session. Some governing bodies of sport specify that the winner in each event plus a number selected at random will be tested.

How will I know if I am selected?
Sportsmen and women selected for testing will be notified by an authorised official. Those selected will be asked to sign a form to acknowledge that they have been notified and agreed to go to the Doping Control Station no later than a stated time. Usually you can go to the Control Station straight away.

Can someone go with me to the Control Station?
You may be accompanied by an appropriate adult (e.g. your team manager or other official). Usually space is limited so that you cannot bring more than one person with you.

What happens at the Control Station?

The Control Station is a quiet place where the sample of urine can be given and bottled and sealed in the correct way.

You will be asked to identify yourself, the collection procedure will be explained, and you will be asked to:

a   choose a set of two numbered bottles from those available
b   give a sample of urine, under supervision
c   enter on the form any medication you have taken in the past three days
d   check and sign that your sample of urine has been placed in the bottles you chose, that the bottles have been sealed and the numbers recorded correctly, and that you have no complaints concerning the collection procedure.

What if I cannot produce the required sample?

Don't worry, plenty of drinks will be available and you will be given plenty of time.

What happens to the samples?

They will be sent to an International Olympic Committee accredited laboratory where they will be analysed.

What types of drugs are banned?

The main classes are:

a   stimulants
b   narcotic analgesics (strong pain killers)
c   anabolic steroids
d   beta blockers (restricted for certain sports)
e   diuretics

In addition there are a number of banned substances which are not covered by the above categories. A list of examples is available from your governing body. This usually corresponds to the list of examples given by the International Olympic Committee.

What happens if no banned substances are found?

Nothing. A negative result will be reported to the governing body of your sport which requested the testing. The samples will then be destroyed.

What happens if a banned substance is found?

The governing body will be informed that a particular substance has been found in your sample of urine. The governing body will then notify you*. In general the procedure is then as follows:

a   you may be suspended from competitions of the governing body while the reason for the presence of the banned substance is considered. For this you* are entitled to:
   (i) a second analysis of the urine sample which you* and a representative may observe
   (ii) attend* with a representative to present your case.
b   a decision will then be taken. This may include suspension from competitions of the governing body for a period
c   you are entitled to appeal against the decision to an authorised body.
* and your parent if you are under 16 years of age.

How can I be safe?

The only completely safe way is to **take no drugs**. Many commonly used medications, whether prescribed by a doctor or purchased at a chemist's, may contain banned substances. If medication is required you should check every medication in advance for the presence of a banned substance and do not take any medication you have not checked. Remember this is **your responsibility**.

Remember your own doctor or chemist may not be aware of the doping regulations for sport so their view on the safety of a medicine may not be correct. A list of examples of banned substances can be obtained from your governing body to show to your doctor. If you have any doubts contact your governing body or the Sports Council for further advice.

What if I need medicine for conditions such as asthma, hay fever or other complaints, but am still fit enough to take part?

There are usually suitable alternative medicines which do not contain banned substances. Your doctor will be able to advise you in the first instance. But remember it is strongly recommended that the composition of the medicine prescribed is checked against the list of examples of banned substances and with your governing body.

How long do drugs stay in my system?

This is extremely variable, depending on the drug and the individual. Some drugs can be eliminated rapidly, while for others, traces can remain for several months.

Can I avoid detection?

No – the sample analysis is extremely sensitive; even trace amounts can be detected and identified.

Is it worth the risk?

No! It may damage your health and your future in sport. In addition, it could endanger the reputation of your sport.

What if I refuse to take the test?

If you are selected for testing but refuse to be tested or do not attend the Control Station as requested, it is considered as though the urine gave a positive test. The procedure above is followed. However, as a sample of urine was not given at the time, there is clearly no chance of a second analysis of the sample.

Couldn't I fill the bottle with someone else's urine?

No – an official will be with you to ensure that the sample is collected in the correct way.

Why can't I have a list of 'safe' drugs?

No list will be complete. New medications come on the market constantly. The substances banned are subject to change.

Note

In most circumstances it is illegal to give any drug to a person under 16 without the consent of a parent. Parental consent is also needed for drug testing in this age group.

Key points

1   Drugs are medicines designed to help the sick and are only prescribed under strict medical control.

2   Some 'over-the-counter' medicines available at chemists for colds, headaches, etc. contain substances that could result in a ban. Check all medicines. There are always acceptable alternative remedies.

3   You will be helped in this by carrying the Sports Council's 'Check Card' to show to your doctor or chemist. It offers treatment guidelines.

4   Protect your health, your sport, your reputation, your family, friends and country. **Do not cheat.**

WEIGHT-LIFTING SAFETY

Safety for teachers and coaches

Every teacher wishes to prevent accidents in physical education. Such accidents have dire consequences: the victims may suffer physical and psychological injury and distress; the P.E. programme may be cut back and restrictions introduced; teachers, coaches and authorities may suffer stress and loss by being sued for negligence and damages if students are injured while using defective equipment, if there was inadequate supervision or if reasonable care was not exercised by the teacher.

Recommendations: general physical education

1 Have all equipment inspected regularly. Report, in writing, all deficiencies in apparatus, mats, floor surfaces, rigs, equipment, etc. to your superior. Don't use them again until they are put right. Obtain the best equipment and maintain it in good condition.
2 Make sure you have taught all the necessary skills, including safety procedures, before requiring students to exercise them in game, class or competition situations.
3 Obtain medical approval before reinstating an injured student into game, class or competition activity. Obtain and follow medical advice.
4 Beginners require special teaching and supervision. A champion attempting an entirely new skill is still categorised as a beginner at that skill. Proper supervision involves being there when needed.
5 Fatigue often precedes accidents. Students must be fit for the work to be attempted. A tired pupil is often accident-prone.

6 Keep the apparatus locked up unless at least three pupils wish to use it.

Recommendations: weight training and lifting

1 Ensure that the layout for the different exercises in the weight-training area is carefully planned. Barbells should not be too close to each other. Use mats under the weights. The transport of equipment requires great care. Horseplay is very dangerous.
2 Check barbells, dumb-bells, stands and benches carefully before use. Make sure all collars are tight and barbells are evenly loaded. Check each time apparatus comes out and after every set.
3 Only train in an area where the floor is even, firm and non-slip. Do not train in bare feet.
4 Check and service the equipment regularly.
5 Coaches should know why and when to teach specific exercises, as well as how. They should also attend an official coaching course.
6 Make sure that two stand-ins are used for all exercises, one each side of the barbell, ready to assist. All pupils must know how to stand-in and catch.
7 Do not attempt limit poundages too soon. Too great a weight will lead to a bad body position which, in turn, may lead to an accident.
8 Exercises must be taught carefully. Strict exercise principles must be employed at all times. Every pupil must advance at his own level.
9 Use only token resistance during exercise learning phases. When muscle groups are weak they lack control. Lack of muscular control can lead to injury. Proceed with caution, always with careful supervision.
10 Correct breathing must be taught on all lifts.

11   Use warm clothing to train in. Fast training procedure will avoid 'local chilling' of muscles.
12   The well-being and safety of lifters comes before personal vanity and ambition.

Safety for pupils and competitors

Weights are impartial apparatus – they make no distinction between beginners and champions. Their use requires careful consideration. The varied skills of the activity must be learned thoroughly. Poor technique, reckless advancement of poundages, irresponsible behaviour – these factors can all cause accidents.

Listen to the coach. Apply the correct training principles, respect the limitations of each individual. Get your mind in shape before starting to train. If you think and behave responsibly, the chances of hurting yourself or anybody else will be greatly reduced.

Recommendations

1   Confidence should not be confused with recklessness; the former is built on knowledge, the latter on ignorance. The only impression reckless weight training makes is on the floor!
2   Although weight training and weight lifting are great fun because you can see and take pride in the progress you are making, to become an expert still takes time – time spent on understanding and mastering each step before moving onto the next. Don't try to run before you can walk.
3   Before trying the next exercise or training plan, obtain and follow advice from your coach. The coach's job is to ensure that all the experiences a lifter will have from the use of weights will be pleasant ones.
4   Never train alone. Always have one stand-in at each end of the bar. Stand-ins should be aware of what you are going to do and when.
5   Keep to your schedule of exercises. Do not advance to poundages without a coach's advice. Do not sacrifice correct body position for poundage.
6   Do not try to keep up with others who may seem to be making more rapid progress than yourself. Train at your own level and within your own capabilities.
7   Horseplay and practical jokes can be very dangerous. If you are not deriving enough enjoyment from serious weight-lifting work, you are using a poor programme.
8   Wear firm training shoes and warm clothing.
9   Check all apparatus before use and after each exercise. Check collars, ensuring that they are secured firmly. Make sure all bars are loaded evenly. Concentrate and be safety conscious.

Appendix A

The British Amateur Weight Lifters' Association

All weight lifting in Great Britain is under the control of the British Amateur Weight Lifters' Association (B.A.W.L.A.) which is affiliated to the International Weight Lifting Federation (I.W.L.F.) and the British Olympic Association (B.O.A.). B.A.W.L.A. is responsible for coaching at all levels and maintains a National Coaching Scheme with a National Coach, assisted by staff coaches, senior coaches, coaches and instructors, and holders of the Leaders Award and the School Teachers Award.

It is the responsibility of the Coaching Committee to ensure that the highest levels of training for lifters are achieved, through the qualification of coaches at the above levels. All lifters are most strongly advised to join an official B.A.W.L.A. club where they will receive first-class coaching by highly qualified coaches who themselves have been trained on the basis of the information in this book. In addition, B.A.W.L.A. is responsible for the training of a corps of referees of the highest standard and integrity and for the adjudication of weight lifting at all levels.

B.A.W.L.A. provides six coaching courses, covering relevant aspects of weight training for fitness, power training for sport, competitive weight lifting and powerlifting and supporting subject matter. These courses, leading to National Coaching Awards, are as follows.

1 Leader Certificate
2 Teacher Certificate
3 Instructor Award – Part I
4 Instructor Award – Part II
5 Coach Award – Part I
6 Coach Award – Part II

Useful addresses

General enquiries
Wally Holland OBE FADO, B.A.W.L.A. General Secretary, 3 Iffley Turn, Oxford, OX4 4DU

Coaching courses
John Lear BA, Dip.PE, Cert.Ed, B.A.W.L.A. Director of Coaching, 'The Willows', 4 Fords Heath, Shrewsbury, Shropshire, SY5 8PZ

Refereeing/technical matters
Ian Thomson, B.A.W.L.A. Technical Committee Secretary, 86 Saughton Road North, Edinburgh, EH12 7JU

APPENDIX B

A charter of conduct

The following is taken from the Central Council of Physical Recreation's (C.C.P.R.) 'A Charter of Conduct'.

Introduction

The laws and rules of sports are established by their governing bodies. The interpretation and application of the rules are in the hands of officials, umpires and referees; but the standards of conduct are set by the competitors and their coaches.

The following Charter calls attention to the urgent need for all the major participants in sport – governing bodies, schools and clubs, coaches and competitors – to reaffirm the factors that constitute good conduct in sport and to strive for the highest ideals of sportsmanship.

Terms of the charter

Governing bodies

1   Must ensure that their rules are fair, thoroughly understood by competitors and officials, and properly enforced.
2   Must make every effort to ensure that the rules are applied consistently and with absolute impartiality.
3   Must make every effort to impress upon participants and officials the absolute need to maintain the highest standards of sportsmanship in the organisation and practice of their sport.

Coaches

1   Must insist that competitors understand and abide by the principles of good sportsmanship.
2   Must not countenance the use of drugs by competitors.
3   Must never employ methods or practices that might involve risks to the long-term health or physical development of their charges.
4   Must not attempt to manipulate the rules to the advantage of their charges.

Competitors

1   Must abide by both the laws and the spirit of their sport.
2   Must accept the decisions of umpires and referees without question or protestation.
3   Must not cheat and in particular must not attempt to improve their performance by the use of drugs.
4   Must exercise self-control at all times.
5   Must accept success and failure, victory and defeat with good grace and without excessive display of emotion.
6   Must treat their opponents and fellow participants with due respect at all times.

Conclusion

In order to bring about the raising of standards of behaviour across the wide spectrum of sport, the C.C.P.R. expects all governing bodies of sport and recreation, clubs, teachers, coaching organisations and spectators to give study to the Charter and take the necessary action to incorporate its relevant principles into their own rules and codes of practice.

INDEX